Book Commissioning and Acquisition

Second edition

'I can't imagine any new editor not gaining an enormous amount from this book, and many experienced commissioning editors too would learn important things. It's clear, detailed, up to date, and honest about the pitfalls and opportunities that confront commissioning editors today, and the qualities they need to deal with them.'
Helen Fraser, *Managing Director, Penguin (UK)*

'This is an excellent guide for all aspiring editorial staff and, indeed, established editors. Gill Davies give a clear and in-depth picture of how to acquire and live with an editorial job-title. Her information is delivered in an authoritive, brisk style with a dash of wry humour and clear enthusiasm for a job which can be both exciting, very rewarding and very nerve-racking. Established editors can also learn from this book and I shall happily recommend it to all the staff I help to train.'
Mary Tapissier, *Director, HR and Training, Hodder Headline Publishing*

'Gill Davies' book has many outstanding qualities. Its single most remarkable feature is balance: it maintains the equilibrum between competing forces, whether the contest is between creative authors and target-bound editors; or between achieving intangible "value-add", and ensuring quality through meticulous detail. The book shows at every turn that the author has lived in the difficult "real world" of an author's aspirations and a company's commercial goals. To understand, even to reconcile these sometimes opposing demands, buy and read Gill's book.'
Richard Balkwill, *Copy Train*

Book Commissioning and Acquisition

Second edition

Gill Davies
City University, London

Routledge
Taylor & Francis Group

LONDON AND NEW YORK

First published 1995 by Blueprint
Reprinted 1996, 2001, 2003
by Routledge

This edition first published 2004 by Routledge
2 Park Square, Milton Park, Abingdon, Oxon OX14 4RN

Simultaneously published in the USA and Canada
by Routledge
270 Madison Avenue, New York, NY 10016

Reprinted 2006, 2007, 2008

Routledge is an imprint of the Taylor & Francis Group, an informa business

© 1995, 2004 Gill Davies

Typeset in Palatino by
Florence Production Ltd, Stoodleigh, Devon
Printed and bound in Great Britain
by MPG Books Ltd, Bodmin

British Library Cataloguing in Publication Data
A catalogue record for this book is available from the British Library

Library of Congress Cataloging in Publication Data
A catalog record for this book has been requested

ISBN 10: 0–415–31788–6 (hbk)
ISBN 10: 0–415–31789–4 (pbk)

ISBN 13: 978–0–415–31788–7 (hbk)
ISBN 13: 978–0–415–31789–4 (pbk)

This book is dedicated to the memory of

David Evans
John Harvard-Watts
Peter Wait

real publishers and inspiring colleagues

Contents

Acknowledgements

Having finally got to the end of writing a book, one turns to the 'Acknowledgements'. Perhaps it is the section that one should write first, as without the mass of people – colleagues, friends, and some who are both – and their help, support, training, good companionship and advice over the years, I should scarcely be in a position to comment on anything very much in publishing let alone write a book about it. In the first edition, I gave thanks to many, and that gratitude firmly remains. A new edition requires yet another roll call of the generous-minded types that, thank heavens, publishing still seems to retain and recruit.

Pride of place in the roll call must go to Elisabeth Tribe of Hodder Arnold. A 'guinea pig' for the first edition, when she was still relatively new to editing, she is now in a position to dispense very good advice to me, which I have seized with relief. Also very generous with their time and their invaluable comments have been Paul Cherry of HarperCollins, Tony Lacey of Penguin, Frania Weaver of Sweet & Maxwell, John Peacock of Macmillan, David Tebbutt of Faber & Faber and Andrew Welham of Dorling Kindersley. Without them, the landscape of the book would have been somewhat barer.

I would also like to thank my colleagues at Routledge. Rebecca Barden and Christopher Cudmore persuaded me to write a second edition. Lesley Riddle, Katharine Ahl and Moira Taylor have all been extremely helpful throughout. Alison Foyle was not only generous but thoroughly sensible in her advice and I am especially grateful for her input. Routledge also sought the advice of other publishers. By the nature of these things, I shall never know who these anonymous advisers were, but I am grateful to them for being rather decent about the first edition, supporting a second edition and giving me lots of good advice about what needed to go in it. I also asked for advice, and was given his usual sound comments, from Richard Balkwill, the publishing consultant and course leader at the Publishing Training Centre. My colleague at City University, Iain Stevenson, has been generous in his support, especially for my need for writing time.

From time to time over a number of years, since our books first appeared in print, I have kept the company of two exemplary and distinguished fellow authors on the Routledge publishing list – Lynette Owen and Hugh Jones. Having supper with them – and just a few drinks – whilst sharing the 'challenges' of writing a book has been a source of entertainment, education and comfort.

Then there are my closest friends. I am much blessed to be surrounded by a bunch of real troopers who have stuck by me through thick and thin. Strictly in order of the length of time I have known them: Elaine Krieger, Ann Mansbridge, the late Hazel Hodgkinson, Jacki Heppard, Carol Smith, Caroline Horsford, Helena Reckitt, Kim Ropek, Frances Harris, Lynn Haywood, Christine Thornborrow, Susan Field, and Pip Pirie.

One character now gone, but who appeared in the Acknowledgements of the first edition, is my cat, Tiddles – a remarkable cat and known to very many publishers as an adornment to any salon and a bit of an adventuress. Fortunately, before she died, she was able to keep tabs on the second edition from a first-class position, sitting on my lap. Her head frequently got in the way of the screen but one was grateful for her interest. Besides, after much exposure to so many publishers over her 16 years, she probably knew more about publishing than many of the industry's current 'experts'.

Since the first edition came out, I confess that what has probably given me the greatest pleasure is seeing the book appear in other languages. It has been translated and published in German, Japanese and Chinese (for Taiwan) and further translations are in preparation for South Korea, mainland China and Poland. I had never expected that the book would be read much beyond the boundaries of London publishing.

That development was exciting, as indeed has been the realisation of how much the book is used in publishing houses and on courses. All of this is due to Vivien James, then of Blueprint, who commissioned the book and played a huge part in its progress. As in the first edition, I reserve my final and greatest thanks for her.

Introduction

1

This is a book about the role of an editor, a position that most people in the publishing industry still regard as the pivotal one. Today, marketing is a powerful and essential part of the publishing process, and there will be few houses where marketing colleagues are not heavily involved in the decision to publish a book. In some trade houses, with a strong commercial edge, marketing may have the final word in that decision.

Editorial still occupies the key territory where most publishing ideas are received, created and then developed before eventually receiving approval for publication. Editors, therefore, are highly influential 'gate-keepers', since it is they who choose which projects will go forward for development and for approval by other colleagues. While the editor remains the prime person in contact with authors, he or she will remain powerful. It is authors who write the books, who more often than not create the ideas, who (often being at the heart of the market for which they are writing) will be closest to the reader, and who are likely to generate the greatest interest and therefore publicity around a book. The author is not only the real creator of the book, he or she is the walking storehouse of information about it and its readers, is the greatest enthusiast for the book but, paradoxically, the person who sometimes has to be nursed or intensely supported. These factors are key to the functions of the editorial role.

WHY BE AN EDITOR?

Being at the interface between the author and what he or she creates is exciting and can be influential. The opportunity to work with an author on content is also highly satisfying. The role is sometimes likened to that of a midwife. Not all authors want or need to have an involved editor, but very many do. Not every book one publishes is going to be a hot property – there will be mid-list books – but when one has the chance to work with an author on a book that makes outstanding sales or is highly influential, then one realises that being an editor is a very privileged job. Indeed, many editors will link growth in confidence to having been involved in such a success. Truthful editors will also confess that they did not always spot that a book was going to be quite so influential. They might have thought the book had something going for it, and merited publication, but perhaps no more than that. It does not matter. They made the right decision and they will learn from the experience. Confidence grows, along with decisiveness.

It is the editor to whom the author's information, enthusiasm, knowledge, demanding behaviour and emotion are addressed. How we receive all that and how we handle it is the reason why the role of editor is so influential. A few editors do not have a fundamental understanding of the importance of their role and, as a consequence, their marketing and production colleagues do not always view editors as positively as they should. It need not be like that. An effective editor demonstrates his or her indispensability every day as a touchstone to others, a resource for information, energy and enthusiasm.

This book is about learning to do one's job properly as an editor. It is a hard job to do, and to do it well requires application and courage – two things that do not necessarily go together. In the past it was thought that the skills of being a good editor could not be taught and the job remained shrouded in a slightly glamorous veil of mystery. Today, editors are sent off with everyone else to learn 'skills'. Those skills are often about finance and investment, marketing and digital technology, and are entirely necessary. They help the editor to see the broader picture, including understanding how one should do one's job in order to meet the aims and objectives of the publishing house.

The skills that are scarcely taught are about how to chase after a good book and a good author; how to spot a viable book idea from some quite general discussions with an author or to see the nugget of a good book within a book outline that might be unsuitable; how to ensure that authors do not deliver their work behind schedule; how to create and develop marketable books; how to persuade authors not to interfere inappropriately in the publishing process; how to build and maintain relationships of mutual professional respect with authors; how to contribute fully to the whole team that is a publishing house.

This book is a systematic attempt to address those things that really make the difference in successful commissioning. It is also about what seem like quite mundane things such as how to keep the various parties who are involved in the process informed and encouraged; how to give help and support so that they can perform to optimum ability and effectiveness. It never loses sight of a fundamental principle, which is: within the walls of a publishing house, it is the editor who 'minds' the book and the success of that book will stand or fall on the ability of that editor to do his or her job well and responsibly. This book will often dwell on what goes wrong, and quite frequently does, because publishing is a profession centred on people (many of them authors) who are often intense and over-endowed with nervous energy because they are creative and bring huge emotional investment to the publishing process; a profession that has at its centre a product that is individual, quirky and demanding like no other mass-produced artefact to be found in the high street. If a good editor is a good motivator and informer, he or she is just as likely to be a good damage limitation expert.

THE STRONGEST AND THE WEAKEST LINK

It is no accident that it is editors who tend to command most private and public attention in and around publishing. Not only do good editors make the difference to the success of a house, they provide tremendous PR interest outside it. They can attract authors with ease because of their reputations. Their conviction and commitment can be a huge galvanising and energising force among the rest of the publishing staff. They are valuable. However, they can also alienate authors and colleagues, and too often it is done behind a surface arrogance that masks fundamental incompetence. What makes authors angry are editors who do a less than adequate job of publishing their books. Some editors seem to get by on charm alone – again, a not entirely satisfactory approach to professionalism.

Publishing appears from the outside to be a comparatively easy profession to be in. Surely it is easy to spot a good manuscript and, after that, one simply has to get the book reviewed and out into the market. Working within publishing we know that is not so but, because our profession does seem an uncomplicated one from the outside, and because it also appears to be a rather enjoyable and interesting one, when we are found lacking, we can be severely criticised. Furthermore, what we have mishandled is the proverbial blood, toil, tears and sweat of a writer who may have worked on a manuscript for a couple of years or more. Being competent is a serious issue for editors and it is more complicated and subtle than simply meeting targets regarding productivity, or learning to understand company accounts, or getting to grips with the skills of marketing or digital technology – all of which are entirely necessary to the gradual broadening and developing of an editor.

There are other factors in play too. Many publishing staff are poorly paid and not well trained. Staff turnover is growing. Many junior-level jobs are vacated every couple of years or so. This brings inherent problems which can be exacerbated by the multi-layered character of publishing. Responsibility is spread over many levels and expertises. This can also be the source of errors and misjudgements if there are weak links in the chain.

What most young editors need when they first start commissioning are not primarily business skills; they want guidance and support on how they go about the central challenge of the job. How do we find good books and authors? Success in business flows from an ability to do that.

This book sets out to do two things. It will present the main principles and practices involved in commissioning work which are necessary if one is going to be at the very least a competent editor. But it will also tackle the 'danger areas', the things we cannot spot coming at us, the things that spell trouble, the things to avoid like the plague. This is the damage limitation aspect of the job, which is essential given the combination of a publishing process that is complex, deadline-orientated, highly labour intensive and yet creative, and involves an added, sometimes volatile, ingredient from outside the publishing house called 'the author'.

Editors need a thorough understanding of both these aspects if they are to be properly useful to the publishing houses where they work. A good grounding builds competence, and competence usually leads to successful publishing. A successful editor is generous with his or her time and effort in respect of authors and colleagues. An editor who gives, receives back commitment, energy and enthusiasm from both.

WORKING WITH RISK AND UNCERTAINTY

It should be stated at the outset that being an editor is not a job for the faint-hearted. Many of us have started out in the profession feeling shy and diffident but somehow have managed to battle on because the shame of failure has actually exceeded the awful gnaw in the pit of the stomach which is called anxiety. To begin with, most young editors think that the scary part of the job is going to be coping with authors who are either hugely famous or successful, or terrifyingly demanding and aggressive, or extraordinarily clever. Thankfully all those characteristics rarely reside in one person. You will also discover that most authors are primarily interested in whether they are going to get on with you or not, and whether you are fundamentally competent.

The truth then dawns that what is really frightening about the job is that the results of your labours are all too public and tend to linger for quite some time. They are called sales figures and reviews. For specialist publishers the results of those labours can remain in the warehouse for too long, giving colleagues every opportunity to analyse your mistakes. But at least the rhythms of specialist publishing allow a title the chance to build up sales over time. For the consumer books editor there is no time to nurse sales; no place for 'sleepers'. The book either moves off the bookshop shelves fast, or it joins the army of returns and contributes to the running total of unearned advances.

Then there are the reviews. How many editors have opened the quality Sunday papers first to have their hearts filled with excitement to see one of their books in the review pages, only to be followed immediately by a tightening of the gut at the split-second thought that the review might be critical. As it is for all performers, the process of being judged in print is a very public one and adds an extra dimension to this particular job in publishing. Only an editor can be judged in this way. No other job in publishing has its effectiveness measured not only through sales but also by public pronouncements.

Many editors do not survive this and leave the industry. Others are repeatedly thrown in the deep end in the understanding that if you are any good, you'll make it to the shore. Alas, those who do make it to the shore will do so with a set of bad habits that are entirely concerned with survival and nothing to do with good publishing practice. Such individuals are often quite damaging to those around them.

Being an editor is not just 'fun' and 'exciting' – two over-used words in our profession. It is also tough and requires rigour and professionalism. Talent is no longer enough. The fun and excitement are there but they tend to come with a sustained understanding of an editor's job and from the pleasure of working in a team involved in a steady stream of successful books. Such momentum is not achieved quickly or easily. It requires persistent application. Job satisfaction can take its time to kick in. Perhaps two or three years will go by before one starts to feel a greater sense of control of one's list and also to see a glimmer of the results of one's labours.

THE ROUTE TO BECOMING AN EDITOR

THE EDITORIAL ASSISTANT

Someone destined to become an editor usually starts out on the very bottom rung of the editorial ladder as an editorial assistant. The new entrant is likely to spend time properly assisting an editor/senior editor/editorial director/publisher. That 'assisting' can indeed entail making telephone calls, filing, booking a restaurant table and ordering tickets for travel, but it is also likely to encompass checking manuscripts, having direct contact with authors, writing copy, getting readers' reports, liaising with other departments, keeping editorial databases up to date, and drawing up contracts. Clearly, from the start, considerable responsibility is involved and one needs to be a good all-rounder, possessing interpersonal, writing and organisational skills.

Over time the assistant is gradually being trained to do many jobs which are ultimately the manager's responsibility but which that overstretched person cannot fit in during a busy day. A manager has to set priorities and delegate. Being an extension of your boss can sometimes seem cramping – you may long for your own autonomy – but it does give an assistant a wonderful front-row seat from which to observe what an editor actually does. Even the most hard-pressed editor wants a break from the real work from time to time in the day to discuss problems, projects, authors, what's happening in other departments, and so on. The assistant is the person he or she is most likely to talk to in the first instance. An assistant can pick up a lot of information not only about being editor but also about publishing. Being an assistant provides you with an excellent grounding. Because of the front-row aspect of the job, it can also provide good opportunities to be noticed and to impress.

Although this is an entry-level job, it is an important one because the increasing workloads of today's editors mean that the editorial assistant has come to play a vital role in the efficient functioning of most editorial departments.

If the assistant does this job well, he or she may be promoted to assistant editor. At this stage autonomy increases. Assistant editors are not likely to be given lists of their own to work on but will be given a discrete part of a list or a particular group of authors. By the nature of things an assistant editor, therefore, is likely to be working alongside a full editor or senior editor on a large list, one big enough to require more than one set of hands. Frankly, the assistant editor is not likely to be given the 'plums' on that list – they will be reserved for the editor – but it is a start from which to build.

THE DEVELOPMENT EDITOR

Another career opportunity *en route* to becoming an editor is to work as a development editor. In many respects the role of a development editor resembles that of an assistant editor, as described above. In textbook publishing, however, a development editor can also take on specific duties which properly encapsulate the word 'development'. The development editor may be asked to research subject areas that could lend themselves to publishing opportunities. The research could entail talking to authors, advisers and book buyers, copious amounts of reading of relevant resources (including government publications that set out new directions in, for example, education), and pulling down data, particularly, these days, off the internet. Working – almost inevitably – in conjunction with a senior editorial colleague, the development editor will produce a set of findings about a subject area which may lead to the emergence of precise publishing ideas that can then be taken forward.

A development editor could also work on projects that are already in the pipeline. Some textbooks are quite complex. A development editor could be assigned to take over the work-in-progress of a textbook in respect of the team of authors who might be engaged in writing it, researching illustrations, doing preparation work ahead of production and design, clearing permissions, and so on. Here the development editor is engaging in an intimate, hands-on involvement prior to the publication process to ensure that the project finally emerges as planned. The development editor is a valuable partner of a senior editorial colleague, allowing him or her to get on with the more proactive work of list development and management.

Although this kind of work is probably more common in specialist publishing, it also exists in consumer publishing, particularly amongst companies that are brand orientated and are highly focused on the interests of their markets.

PROGRESSION TO EDITOR

Having demonstrated competence and achievement at these levels, the next step up is into the role of full editor. There is nothing automatic about this process. You may not be able to progress up the ladder in the house in which you work, simply because a job is not available at the time. You may have to move to another house in order to be promoted. Jobs are sometimes created for exceptional people because the company is determined to keep them. Usually it is because it is possible to combine the newly created job with a publishing opportunity. Let's say that an editorial director has been nurturing ideas about starting a theatre list. The presence of a bright and energetic person with known enthusiasm for and knowledge of theatre studies might just persuade the editorial director that the time has come to build such a list, and a new editorial role is created. Opportunity has combined on both levels.

Secondly, competence and achievement do not necessarily lead to advancement to the role of editor. You may well demonstrate competence at one level but there may be question marks hanging over your ability to operate at the level above. In particular the resources required of an editor are exceptional energy, good judgement, strong nerves, an ability to concentrate both on a broad level and on small details, to be curious about everything to do with publishing, and to possess good social skills. Publishing houses are not looking for paragons but do need people who score highly on most of the attributes just listed. Furthermore, those who are good at 'assisting' are not always so good at going it alone.

There are other routes into editorial work. In the past, there was more of a strict demarcation between the main departments of a publishing house, with few people crossing from one to another. Gradually that has broken down with the realisation that career experience in marketing, including sales, can equip some people with the credentials for becoming successful editors. Indeed, working in marketing and sales is a very good way of gaining experience *en route* to becoming an editor. This experience is just as relevant to making judgements about books as is experience solely gleaned in an editorial department.

Production colleagues seem to cross into editorial less frequently, presumably because these colleagues have far less direct contact with the market and because, for many of them, the technical or craft challenge of making books can be an end in itself. Experience and flair in the production of highly illustrated books, however, can form the basis of an editorial career in that type of publishing, where attention to detail, and good grasp of layout and design, are fundamental to a book's success in the market-place.

COMPETITIVE ENTRY

The greatest hurdle for many people is simply that of getting into publishing to begin with. The publishing world is a relatively small one compared with other industries and therefore the entry process is a highly competitive one. Some will get jobs after graduating from university (the possession of a degree is an almost inevitable qualification for would-be entrants for editorial work) by applying for an advertised job and impressing the employer during a series of interviews. The lucky ones make it in one step.

As preparation for a career in publishing, some graduates undertake further study on publishing degree courses. There are some notable and well-established courses in the UK and North America. This is a sensible move since these courses give students a broad-ranging and in-depth education in all aspects of publishing. Students are also likely to get exposure to experienced professionals who teach on these courses or act as guest lecturers. Many of these courses include job placements for a number of weeks at reputable publishing houses, which can sometimes lead to permanent employment. This is the kind of experience that an employer is looking for when recruiting. More information on courses is shown at the end of the book. Nevertheless, even these graduates, who by then will have developed a considerable knowledge base, must come to terms with the fact that they may have to apply several times before they get their first job in publishing. Generally speaking, it is more helpful to be able to show evidence of a desire to enter publishing – for example, working occasionally in a bookshop, or going on a publishing course – than a simple, expressed love of books.

It is nothing less than hard grind and luck comes into it too. Publishers are often asked for advice from people trying to get into editorial work and finding they are getting nowhere. They have to point out that there are no easy fixes and some will simply have to live with their disappointment and consider another career. On the other hand, other courses of action can be recommended. For example, working for a literary agent or in bookselling can provide a route into publishing. Both of these options can provide valuable experience which is very closely related to the work that goes on in publishing houses and is the kind of thing that an employer's eyes pick out when scrutinising CVs.

Occasionally, publishers recruit people into editorial work who have gained experience in different, but related, spheres. For example, university teachers sometimes become academic editors; or school teachers become educational editors; or lawyers can become legal editors. In this instance these people are being recruited because of their in-depth knowledge of that particular market or subject area. Candidates with the kind of expertise that is essential to electronic publishing are clearly attractive to publishers in scientific, technical and medical publishing. In this instance, the employer needs to be convinced that the recruits can make the adjustment from one completely different world to another and have good commercial sense and drive because the adjustment is a very big one.

Whatever the route in, it will be a highly competitive one. Nepotism exists in publishing, as elsewhere, but is on the decline compared with the past. The industry is such a broadly competitive place, and nowadays often operating within difficult economic environments, that publishers have to be absolutely sure they are recruiting the best on offer which means taking a good look at everything on offer, not just being content to take on 'a bright young thing' with connections.

STRUCTURE OF THE BOOK

Each chapter is designed to take the reader through the main functions of being a commissioning editor. It cannot hope to cover every single task that is required of an editor, but it does cover all the basic processes and skills that are common to all book publishing. Each chapter also covers things that can go wrong. Most training in editorial work focuses on teaching the basic functions and skills that will be expected of you. It will hint at what can go wrong, implicitly, by teaching you that you must negotiate contracts properly, that you must get your manuscripts delivered on time, that you must cost your books carefully, and so on. It is unlikely to tackle in any real depth the consequences that follow from any of these things rolling out of control. The nature of teaching is that it 'is designed to help you do something in a positive, proactive sense. It seldom teaches you 'damage limitation', as referred to earlier: i.e. if 'x' were to befall me, what would I do to cope?

Understanding damage limitation really only comes from the experience of dealing with the unexpected, the unplanned. Each chapter therefore attempts to distil some of the most common 'accidents waiting to happen' in editorial work. Not all of them are covered; only the most often encountered. If you find yourself stuck with something, do not waste time sweating it out. Get some advice from the most experienced colleague on hand – *quickly*. There are also case studies at the end of each substantive chapter. Chapters 8, 9 and 10 are more reflective.

TERMINOLOGY

One of the most tricky aspects that has emerged during the writing of this book has been the fact that each publishing house uses its own particular terminology. Furthermore, terminology differs not just from house to house but from country to country, so the terms which are used in this book are explained below.

COMMISSIONING EDITOR

The person responsible for evaluating typescripts, proposals, projects; for creating ideas for new books and developing them; for contracting authors; for seeing books through the publishing process. In some companies this person is called the 'publisher' if he or she is responsible for a very large list or several lists.

In North America the role is given the name of 'acquisitions or acquiring editor'. This book is about the functions and skills of that particular person, whatever title we attach to him or her.

Commissioning editors are frequently referred to as 'editors', both in this book, and especially by authors. A commissioning editor is not a sub-editor – the person who works on the detail of manuscripts (also known as typescripts!) and proofs.

BUDGETS

Rather perversely this does not mean how much money you, the editor, have to spend, but how much money you are supposed to make for your company. Your company may refer to it as a 'revenue plan'. Depending on when your company's financial year occurs, at some point in the calendar year editors are asked to forward to the editorial director/publisher/managing director/financial director (whoever has responsibility for budgeting in your company) a list of books that you fully expect to publish in the following financial year. This list is annotated by size of print run, number of sales expected in the home and export markets in the first year of the book's life, price or prices if you are doing a dual edition, other significant income for subsidiary rights, and average discounts that will apply.

Happily, a software program is likely to crunch through the numbers and all the variables and come up with a sum of money, i.e. the total revenue that your books are likely to achieve in that year if all goes to plan. Succinctly, the budget is your target for the number of titles and revenue for the following year. Management fully expects editors to meet their budgets. Whatever this budgetary process is called in your company, it is the key criterion by which an editor's effectiveness is measured.

PROFIT AND LOSS ACCOUNT

Again this can be known by other names, for example as a 'project evaluation', and rather misleadingly as 'costings'. Essentially in this exercise the projected sales revenue for a book is set down, from which are deducted production costs and royalties to end up with a figure which is called the gross profit. Some companies deduct other costs, such as distribution and sales, before they arrive at their gross profit. Wherever the line is drawn, it should produce a percentage figure of profit which senior management believes necessary for the financial good health of the company. Your line manager will make you aware of your company's desired gross profit figure. It is highly likely that the company for which you work provides software that will allow you to create spreadsheets showing income and costs.

Whatever names and procedures your company follows, you will be taught them. An editor has a right to demand clear guidance from management, especially in the areas of procedures and targets. These are the questions you should be asking:

- What does the company expect of me in respect of the kinds of book it wants me to publish, the number of titles in any given year, and the target revenue? Has it stipulated a minimum level of profit and revenue for the titles I acquire?

• What training will I be given on the job and out of house to ensure that I am fully informed about the company's procedures and objectives and which will enable me to develop and meet expectations?

ONE SIZE FITS ALL?

No book on editorial skills could hope to encapsulate all the demands, challenges and practices of all editorial work. We all have our specialisms. We are working to different markets and we focus our publishing practice to fit our particular needs. But there is a core aspect to editorial work that is remarkably consistent right across the publishing spectrum. We have more in common than we sometimes realise. We have authors in common and sometimes we discover when we talk to colleagues in other areas of the industry that a successful novelist can behave rather similarly to a judge-turned-author or an academic with a series of influential books behind him or her. The process of writing for publication can create the same crises of confidence regardless of the subject matter.

We also have process in common. Again, the intimacies of process might differ across the publishing spectrum, but essentially editors are engaged in the same activity: contracting books, hauling them in as close as possible to delivery date, steering them through the publication process, and ensuring that everything is done to achieve maximum sales in the market. This book is about what we have in common.

How to choose what to publish

2

In this chapter we shall be looking at the following issues:

- factors that affect the author's choice of publisher
- the characteristics of a successful author
- book proposals
- whether the book fits your list
- what exactly is the readership and how to reach it
- using appropriate advisers and assessing their advice carefully
- consulting colleagues for their views
- ensuring you have all the information you need and have properly examined it
- working with literary agents
- being prepared to resolve conflicts between intuition and facts when making publishing decisions

How editors choose books to publish remains the most mysterious question for people outside publishing and, indeed, for those inside who never get a proper glimpse of the process. Like many mysteries, however, it can be reduced to fairly prosaic levels, although some books do escape the process of rational choice. Most editors will happily admit that there were some titles that they published with success in the face of evidence that suggested an outcome to the contrary. Even specialist publishers, who work with fairly well-defined ideas about what books are required reading for their market, will own up to having published titles that did not fit into, for example, any course-reading requirement, but were titles that intuition told them that they should publish.

These books are the exception to the rule. Most books fit into a tried and tested pattern both in what they have to say and in terms of the market need they are fulfilling. The truth is that very few authors have the ability to write something truly original that sweeps the board. Editors who have been lucky enough to spot the highly unusual and successful, with hindsight tend to forget the sleepless nights and anxiety experienced at the time they decided to back the unknown. Nevertheless, these editors deserve our respect because they have something immensely important and valuable: judgement and the courage to back it.

Very few editors are required to choose what to publish completely in isolation from other factors. They work within the context of a list, whether it is a cookery list, or a fiction list, or a legal list, or a history list. In any publishing house considerable knowledge has been built up over a number of years about what is suitable for publication within that list, as have well-formed ideas about what constitutes a particular type of book that tends to sell. Editors in most strands of publishing – whether consumer books or specialist – are able to identify a genre of book and to make comparisons between the example on offer and similar books already published with sales records which can be examined for signs of potential for the yet unpublished.

Then there is the author. A new author obviously presents difficulties. He or she does not yet have a track record. Those who have published before, however, can be scrutinised for their likely ability either to produce another winner, or a mere bread-and-butter, mid-list item that will just get by. Authors have followings too; even specialist ones have fans and that factor can simply be enough for the editor to choose to go with him or her again.

The selection process is two-way. Both authors and publishers go through the process of selecting each other.

HOW AUTHORS SELECT PUBLISHERS

From the point of view of the authors, they are seeking a house whose lists and marketing they admire. The two are almost inseparable because, viewed from the outside, the successful house appears to have a knack not only of choosing prime material to publish, but also of sending strong messages to the market-place that this is content the buyer is going to want or need, or both. Furthermore, those publishers' books are readily available to the buyer. They can be found in the bookshops or there are efficient systems that allow the buyer to get them direct from the publisher, or they can be bought through the internet. Authors want good editorial and production standards from their publishers but they also need to feel secure that their books will *reach* the reader.

To be more specific, what is likely to be going through authors' minds when they are thinking about choosing a publisher?

- *Cachet* – that undeniable element that can intrigue authors, the prospect of being on a list that currently seems to have the most exciting writers, whatever their field. They want to be part of all that.
- *Brand identity* – this is not that common in publishing but there are examples of publishing lists whose identity is linked so strongly with a certain kind of book that it is immediately recognisable; for example, Dorling Kindersley. This brand identity can be linked with physical appearance or with content. In these cases, customers purchase the books because they feel they know what they are buying.
- The presence of *an editor of demonstrable flair and judgement* – authors talk to each other and they both recommend and advise against working with certain editors. The word gets around. The editor can become recognised for being good at certain things. Choosing successful books; working creatively and sympathetically with authors; ensuring that books get good production and design treatment; being good at galvanising marketing and promotion to deliver the appropriate campaign which leads to sales – these are the kinds of attributes (usually a mixture of all of them) that bring recognition and authors to editors. Some authors (especially fiction writers) regard the editor as so important to them that it is the key issue guiding choice. These authors are conscious of a need to work with someone with whom they can have a supportive and sympathetic relationship, which helps them when writing. Some high-profile authors have moved house (in lucrative deals) but only on the condition that the editors at their former publishers still edit their future books.
- *High-profile promotion and marketing* – the authors have evidence that the publishing house has fast, reliable distribution; has attractive point-of-sale materials; has a successful PR department that delivers campaigns that command wide attention; promotes directly and in a focused way to specialist buyers, for example.
- *Production* – the publisher produces well-designed books with production values the author likes.
- The publisher has made a significant commitment to developing product through *digital technology*, which the author knows will be attractive to the proposed readership.

For some authors there might be another consideration, and that is the size of the house. There is some evidence, in both consumer books and specialist publishing, of authors choosing to publish with smaller, independent houses because they want to feel they are getting individual treatment and fear getting lost in the big programmes of the large companies. When they become established as successful authors, it is likely that they will gravitate to bigger houses, where there is spending power and where the author no longer has to fight for space.

HOW EDITORS SELECT AUTHORS

When editors choose authors, they have one main objective in mind. They are looking for authors whose books are going to sell successfully. In practice, this process of selection might work through the following ways.

COMMISSIONING

- In a proactive fashion an editor approaches authors with an established track record and presents them with good publishing ideas, in the hope of attracting them away from their existing publisher and signing them up.
- The editor, again, comes up with the subjects and ideas and looks for an acknowledged expert to fill the writing role. Sometimes these experts have no prior experience of writing books. Here the editor is prepared to take the risk that the lack of writing experience (and, in all likelihood, skills) can be more than compensated for by the grasp of subject the author brings and that the editor (and a good sub-editor) will be able to help the author put the book in good shape.
- Sometimes editors present ideas for books that the authors reject, but as a result of the discussions they have had, new ideas emerge which lead to something tangible.
- Occasionally editors will spot something in print, but perhaps in a restricted form (materials produced for public sector employees, for example), and will use the ideas in that material as a starting-point for creating something more ambitious.

ACQUIRING

Editors of course select authors as part of the process of accepting submissions. When editors examine proposals for publication, they will take factors regarding the author into consideration: for example, qualification for the task; reputation in a subject area or field; evidence of writing ability; track record; and so on. This will be dealt with later in the chapter.

Authors who are likely to be successful tend to have certain characteristics. They

- understand the market for the book
- know their subject
- know how their books score over the competition
- are able to connect with the reader
- write well

These characteristics are likely to become apparent when you look through their proposals and will be confirmed by the opinions of your advisers, if you are a specialist publisher, or by your publishers' readers if you work in consumer publishing.

CONTEXT FOR CHOOSING

Just as it would be difficult, if not downright unusual, for any editor to be commissioning books in isolation from what is going on in the rest of the publishing house, it would be pointless for the editor to be commissioning without constant reference to the market to which the books are addressed. Editors must keep themselves in tune with readers' interests and needs. Certainly, that aspect is directly dealt with during the evaluation of specific proposals, but it must be constantly addressed on a broader level if editors are to know what the market wants.

Then there are also the proposals themselves. To begin with, the mass of publishing proposals with which the editor is presented do seem to represent a set of interrelated anxieties which cannot be differentiated one from another. Within a relatively short period of time, however, experience will enable the construction of a set of criteria with which to make some sense of what is on offer. Choosing books to publish is just like any other test of observation; beginning with developing an eye, a feel, a set of navigational tools for getting around. Experience simply heightens and focuses your sense of observation. You learn.

GATHERING MARKET INFORMATION

Depending on the kind of publishing you work in, keeping on top of the market and gauging its needs could mean:

* reading scholarly journals, trade magazines or the national newspapers
* making regular contact with literary agents
* attending conferences
* scrutinising other publishers' catalogues
* reading reviews
* attending literary 'events'
* travelling around universities and schools
* spending time in the bookshops with the reps
* making regular contact with professional bodies
* doing market research

In addition, listening to the radio and watching television as much as possible wherever it relates to specific interests is essential. Ideas and information can come from all directions and should always be absorbed in case it turns out to be useful. There was once a very distinguished editor who read the newspapers from cover to cover every day because he reckoned that he could always extract at least two good ideas worth following. Similarly, a literary agent was heard being thoroughly dismissive of a publisher who admitted in a rather high-minded fashion that he never watched television. She took the view that since he was a consumer books publisher, he had no business cutting himself off from something that the bulk of the population regularly indulged in. He was likely to miss something that people were actually interested in.

TRUE COMMISSIONING WORK

Sometimes editors (along with colleagues) will have an exact idea for a book, series of books or project they would like to publish. They have already done whatever research they require to establish the desirability or need for this book, who will buy it, what format it should be in, what price, and how it will be marketed. The next critical step is to find the right author or authors, hold a series of meetings, which will certainly involve marketing and production, and then contract the book. Detailed discussions will take place over length, delivery date, royalties or fees. In the focus of everyone's mind will be the specific market need that the book is designed to meet and keeping to it. Basically, this is describing the building of a book in a calculated fashion. Market research and publishing have combined absolutely. The editor and colleagues are market-driven and not market-led.

This kind of work is most commonly found in educational publishing. While the books are in preparation they tend to be called projects, signifying the scale of the enterprise and the fact that teams of people work on them. Publishers serving this market inform themselves thoroughly about curriculum needs, they consult endlessly with hand-picked advisers (including working teachers), they choose very carefully authors who know how to write to the market level, and test and retest material. The timing for launching these books is exact. Nothing is left to chance. The cost of getting these projects off the ground is very high. If they succeed, the revenues will be correspondingly satisfactory.

Project publishing of this sort is not unique to educational publishing. It is also found in textbook publishing and reference publishing, but educational publishing is where it has been most widely developed.

Commissioning work can also take less ambitious forms. It can simply mean that the editor has a good idea for a book, finds the right author and then invites (and pays) him or her to write it (having secured the support of colleagues, of course). In essence, the editor has taken a proactive role in the genesis of a book. This kind of work is central to the activity of non-fiction consumer books editors for whom creating publishing ideas for books which can be implemented constitutes a major part of their jobs.

For much of the time, editors in specialist publishing may be less pro-active, although they go out into the market-place (schools, colleges and universities) looking for ideas and good authors to write them up. As a result they receive authors' ideas, proposals, and manuscripts and set to work on them; work that is creative, imaginative and participative.

For much of their time, however, editors in all types of publishing are on the receiving end of ideas and proposals and the rest of this chapter will be devoted to how they evaluate what comes across their desks.

EVALUATING BOOKS AND PROJECTS

It is fairly rare these days to be sent a whole typescript for consider-ation. Most authors prefer, or are requested, to send in an outline synopsis or a treatment for a book. This usually consists of:

- a description in general terms of what the book will be about
- a more detailed description of the content of each chapter
- factual information about length and writing time needed
- a readership evaluation
- an analysis of why the book will be attractive to the prospective reader
- a strengths-and-weaknesses evaluation of the proposed book in rela-tion to any competitive books in print or known to be in preparation – desirable, but not always included
- the author's qualifications to write such a book

Sometimes authors simply send an exploratory letter in advance without the commitment of the outline. In some of the larger publishing houses, editors are then encouraged to send authors a standardised submission form in which the author is asked to provide information about the proposed book under headings which the house considers most relevant to its decision to publish or not. Not all authors will respond favourably to being circumscribed in this way but at the very least, a set of highly focused questions (usually about the market) will help the author think more carefully about the sales potential of his or her book.

Whichever way the author chooses to approach the editor in the first place, the majority of authors will not commit themselves to writing a whole book (unless it is first-time fiction) until they are pretty sure that they have a captive publisher for it.

There are various things to consider when looking at a proposal.

COVERING LETTERS

What does the author's covering letter tell you about him or her? A letter that is literate, well presented, persuasive and realistic in its claims is likely to suggest to the editor that he or she is dealing with someone who is intrinsically a good communicator and therefore stands some chance of being an effective writer. Authors who write letters that are offputting should be quietly avoided. If you don't care for their letters, why should you care for their books? If they have taken trouble with their covering letter then they will probably take trouble over what they write.

CONSTRUCTION OF THE PROPOSAL

Inexperienced editors can become quite anxious about their ability to judge proposals in subjects in which they are not expert. What is required here, however, is not necessarily deep knowledge but simply the ability to look at the construction of the proposal and to ask oneself if it makes sense. You might ask yourself:

• Does the proposal hang together logically?
• Have arguments been marshalled in a coherent way?
• Has the author provided you with factual information that informs his or her ideas or theories?
• If you are examining a proposal for a novel, even at this stage is there good evidence of a robust narrative?

Whatever your subject area, at this stage you are being asked to bring some critical thought and analysis to the submission that is before you – no more than that. Such a process is something you go through, without thinking of it, in your everyday reading habits!

If the outline has been put together with evident careful thought and planning, the chances are that this will work its way through to a similarly well-written and presented book. If the author's 'thread' is difficult to follow then what chance does this person stand with 50,000 words or more at his or her disposal? Early signs of sloppiness are not encouraging.

WILL IT FIT INTO MY LIST?

'Your book is not quite suitable for our list' remains the most popular reason offered to authors for rejecting a proposal. Quite often the editor is trying to be kind by not spelling out the real reasons for refusing a book.

Fitting into a list is a perfectly right and proper consideration for any editor to have in the forefront of his or her mind. It is not simply a matter of not taking on novels when the main thrust of your publishing is cookery books; or suddenly deciding to publish a sociology book when you are normally devoted to law publishing. Those are extreme examples but not entirely unheard of. What is at issue here is the process of acquiring books that have broadly similar markets. This is because publishers build up a reputation for publishing a certain type of book, which is useful when it comes to selling them, and indeed, acquiring them.

The whole question of lists and list building is dealt with in Chapters 6 and 7 in greater detail but, before moving on, what is a list?

THE PUBLISHING LIST

To define a list is quite difficult because it can be both narrow and broad in conception. For example, a fiction list is a broad category and a sociology list is by comparison a narrow one. Here the categories are measured in absolute terms by size and variety of output and market. However, within both categories it is possible to focus down and define the list in a much narrower way. It is possible to be a fiction publisher but only publish historical novels, or be a sociology publisher and only publish first-year undergraduate textbooks.

In practice publishers do define themselves within the broad and narrow categories. For example, companies such as Cape and Faber will publish quite a wide range of literature but it is quite clear from their output that they have defined their lists to encompass high-quality, original writing for the 'serious' reader – a comparatively narrow category. Hodder Arnold is a textbook publisher producing books for a variety of specialist markets. It has, by and large, confined itself to textbook publishing, perceiving its lists as providing material that meets the needs of students with clearly defined educational course requirements. Here again, therefore, is a mixture – a narrow (i.e. specialist) category of publishing but one that provides books for a broad category of readers within that specialism.

What links all these examples and helps towards the definition of a list, is the readership and, most pertinently, the level of readership. There are many examples of levels of readership for novels, from those who love Philip Roth to those whose preference is for Jilly Cooper, including some who are happy with both. It is true that there are professors of philosophy who like to relax with a good detective story or thriller and there are professors of English literature who (under pen names) write them.

Lists organise themselves around a core market. First, take the subject matter – gardening, poetry, geography, computing, teaching, cookery or whatever. Then take the reader – professional, scholarly, pick-up buyer, enthusiast or student. Putting them together establishes the groundwork for developing a product to meet a particular need or want. In addition, there is a need to assess whether there are enough readers out there to make the provision of that product, and at that particular level, worthwhile, i.e. forces of supply and demand.

Clearly, marketing factors play a huge part in the thinking behind list development. All resources in publishing are scarce, even in marketing. It makes far better sense to spread the cost of marketing over a whole family of books that bear some relation to one another than to have to reinvent a whole new marketing strategy with every new, and disparate, book.

This essentially is what a list is all about:

- It reflects a perceived need or want for a product that covers a subject, field of interest, or leisure activity.
- It has readers who are prepared to buy it if it is presented at a level that meets their needs or wants.
- That same readership also has expectations of the product being supplied in particular formats and at prices which the readers find attractive or acceptable.

There is a degree of coherence operating around the notion of supply and demand which emerges in practice in a list: the books 'hang together'; they bear some relation to each other even if that relation is quite broad. The novels of Milan Kundera and A. S. Byatt are by no means similar but they share the common characteristic of being 'serious' literature for which there is a readership.

What makes publishing so interesting to work in, and is the source of its diversity, is the fact that there are so many levels of potential reader for so many subjects. The lists which emerge as a result of that diversity should still possess coherence and identity, both in content and market.

READERSHIP

Many authors claim a far greater potential readership for their books than is realistic. Indeed, what the author states to be the readership for the book, and why, is something to scrutinise very carefully. If the author does not have a well-understood perception of his or her reader, you have grounds to suspect the book will fail.

GUIDELINES ON ASSESSING READERSHIP

1 If the author has not specified the readership fully, ask for a profile.
2 Get the author to analyse the profile in terms of perceived demand. For example, if offered an undergraduate text in biology, ask the author to match the proposed content with course content and demonstrate a strong connection between the two.
3 Make sure, if the book is aimed at a particular level of readership, that the author is not making claims for a market at a higher or lower level. For example, some authors are prone to claim that textbooks are suitable for the top end of the schools market and undergraduates. They sometimes are, but often are not.
4 Get the author to supply statistical evidence to back claims if there are any doubts about market size. For example, authors often talk about a 'growing market'. It may seem growing to them because they are part of a network of enthusiasts engaged in pushing a field or subject area. They have a biased view. Even if the market is growing, has it grown big enough to publish into?
5 Ask the author to specify what the readership is reading now. Are there established and competitive books in print? What's wrong with them? Why is this one better? Get the author to spell this out in detail. Answers that broadly state 'those books aren't any good' are useless but ever present. A strengths-and-weaknesses analysis of the other books is needed, combined with demonstrable evidence of how the author's book will overcome the weaknesses of the others.
6 If the author claims that 'this is the first book on the subject', push for evidence of that. Authors are adept at making claims for originality. Supplement your work with the author by some research – talking to colleagues (especially reps), scrutinising competitors' catalogues, asking your advisers, looking around the bookshops. If the author turns out to be right, then there is a crucial question to ask: if there hasn't been a book on the subject before, is it because there isn't a demand for it? You have to be careful here. There might be a demand that no one has spotted yet.
7 If the book does appear to meet the criteria just outlined, will it be written at a length and in a format that will allow you to price the book to the market? If it's too long, and therefore expensive to produce, the market may reject it on price grounds – unless this new book can replace several which the readership has been buying and using to date.
8 Is there evidence that the author can write for the level of readership? If the author has a track record, you may not be concerned with this question. In the absence of that, sample chapters are essential

when considering a book designed to meet the needs of a market quite precisely. Great cooks do not necessarily make great cookery writers. Have you seen enough specimen chapters to be convinced that the reader can follow and understand the instructions, feels confident following them, and what's more feels motivated to cook the dishes?

9 Finally, what evidence is available from inside and outside your publishing house?

(a) What sales records are there for similar books?

(b) Is there feedback from reps reporting that booksellers would love to see a book on a particular topic because customers are always asking for one?

(c) What market intelligence may be gleaned from keeping up with events; for example, noting government initiatives or European Union regulations that might have an impact on your market and influence your views about what to commission?

(d) Is there evidence from the media of a real growing interest in a subject, field or leisure activity? You might have seen statistical evidence to back this up or your professional association might have released figures showing increasing numbers of book-buyers in particular categories.

(e) Have you noticed the formation of new journals in a particular subject? This is a pretty reliable indicator of a growing interest in a field.

(f) The second or third edition of a book by a competitor is also a good guide to strong sales in that subject area.

(g) Has a professional organisation started doing its own publishing? If so, they may have good insider information indicating potential demand for publications.

(h) Has an exceptionally high turn-out for a conference indicated a growing area of interest in a subject?

When all this has been assessed, you can feel confident that you have answered thoroughly the question 'Who will want to read this book?'

Having done this, if you are genuinely publishing in a new area for the first time, with no existing sales figures to help, a sensible view of the real size of the market is needed. At this point you inevitably have to reach for statistics. Statistics can provide figures from which to make intelligent extrapolations. If it is found that the total potential market is 2,000 readers, quite frankly, some pretty hard justification is required for its publication – unless it is 'must have' information for which this particular niche market will pay a high price.

COMPETITION

Examining what your competitors do is absolutely essential in areas such as textbook or reference publishing, where competitors engage head-on. Even those who work in less focused publishing will take their competitors into consideration when choosing what to publish.

When assessing the competition, what must be looked for in addition to what was covered under the section on readership?

GUIDELINES ON COMPETITION

Pricing

One must aim to match competitors' pricing. If your book is going to be more expensive, it must come with extra benefits to the reader – enhanced content or superior illustrations, for example – over the competitive text. Some years ago, a former school teacher set up his own list, publishing social science textbooks for the schools market. He published out of his own home, keeping the stock in his garage. The content of the books was good – he knew his subject and his market. Being free of the usual overheads, he was able to price his books very cheaply and they sold extremely well. When conventional publishers witnessed this success and decided to enter the field, they had to price their books to match his, therefore living with low profits. This was absolutely necessary because no one felt they could beat him on content. They had to hope that their superior marketing would eventually drive his lists out. His fate was a common one. He threw his lot in with a large publisher who made him a good offer.

Marketing

Are your competitors' promotion and sales campaigns comparable or are they superior? If the latter is the case then why is this so and what can your company do to match it? If matching it is not going to require anything out of the ordinary, but simply a more sustained and widespread application of marketing resources (e.g. more copies being mailed on the inspection copy scheme, extra numbers of review copies, higher than average advertisement spend, bigger lists for direct marketing), then you can proceed, but in the knowledge that you have to make that bigger effort and live with higher costs. Ultimately, of course, it is the marketing department who will make the decision on a higher spend. It will be your job to persuade them. However, if the book needs marketing resources which are unavailable, proceed with care. If your competitor's books sell well because they use a team of college reps marketing direct to the grass roots, and you do not, how can you compete with that?

Compatibility

Even more risky is taking on competitors in an area where you are not properly established. For example, some years ago an academic house was offered a textbook in psychiatry, specifically aimed at the medical market, a market in which they had only a slim tangential presence but where there were several large and successful publishers extremely well versed in the particular demands of promoting and selling to that sector. The book should have failed because it is often dangerous to dabble in areas without having the appropriate resources and the expertise readily available. The book in fact succeeded because it had a Unique Selling Point. It contained a card which the buyer could remove and put in his or her top pocket. The card showed guidelines for on-the-spot diagnoses of patients being admitted to psychiatric hospitals. It also happened to be a very good textbook in its own right but the buyers loved the card and the book knocked the competitive texts off the shelves. This is unusual – experimentation in incompatible markets is risky.

Output

It is often said, 'If there are already 20 books in print on first-year economics/Indian cookery/car mechanics/patio gardening, then publish the 21st.' By and large, output does bear a strong relation to demand. When there is established demand, succinctly, it has one consequence: your book has more titles to compete against. Therefore, nail your unique selling point and, at the very least, match the marketing of competitors.

USING ADVISERS

Specialist publishers do not make decisions on the projects under review without taking professional advice. Trade publishers have teams of very experienced 'readers' who have a good eye for their type of literature. After all, few could possibly find the time to read carefully all the projects and typescripts that are submitted – you need help. The role of the adviser is more important than just helping out. In specialist publishing it is the professional reader who knows the subject area in great depth; who can really follow the arguments that will be presented in a book; who knows the content of courses on which the book would be used; who knows why this book will fill specific needs which the buyer will be able to perceive; who knows if there are other competitive texts either in print or in preparation.

A good adviser will know all these things and will give you a frank opinion on the material under offer. However experienced or knowledgeable specialist publishers become in relation to the fields they publish, they should never forget that if they were really expert, they would be out there in the field; they wouldn't be publishers. Occasionally it is possible to come across editors making their own judgement on content without specialist advice and it shows in the quality of the books they publish.

Advisers, good ones, are valuable people and once found should be cared for and paid properly. The happiest position to be in is having a 'stable' of advisers who are very familiar not only with the market but also with you, your list and how you work. These are people whom you are likely to meet several times over a year. Showing your appreciation by taking them to lunch or paying a small retainer is a sensible thing to do. Occasionally there will be disagreements, and occasionally there can be mistakes when trying out an adviser for the first time but, by and large, they should be taken very seriously. Occasionally advisers will display prejudices and you should keep a watchful eye open for extravagant reports – either positive or negative – from advisers. They usually indicate that judgement is being influenced by something other than the content of a proposal. Remember that good advisers will not only give you sound opinions on the material you send to them but are likely to tip you off about potential authors and provide you with introductions.

How do you find an adviser?

GUIDELINES ON FINDING ADVISERS

- Start at your own back door – ask colleagues and authors; they often have names to suggest.
- Use successful authors – they may be publishing with you or another house. By and large authors have no objection to giving advice to editors in other houses (and sometimes they can end up being one of your own via this route). In any case, do not be put off from approaching the most successful ones first. You will be surprised at just how many are happy to help.
- If you travel around universities, colleges or schools, or attend conferences and exhibitions, note carefully people whom you judge could be suitable advisers.
- If you are a professional publisher, find out the names of people with 'clout' or authority in a particular profession. Especially useful are those with responsibility for setting standards for training and accreditation.
- Note the names of people who frequently appear in the media talking or writing with conviction on subjects where they possess knowledge and expertise. They can range from opera reviewers to journalists

specialising in a subject such as economics or the environment, to the leaders of pressure groups. There is a well-known 'agony aunt' who for years has given valuable advice on books about the psychological distress of illness to a distinguished academic and professional publisher, based on the experience of dealing with her postbag.

Be prepared to call and write around. Your efforts will eventually be rewarded. People like being asked to give advice – they often feel flattered. Always agree on a date for getting a report from them and a fee, and assure them that the adviser's name will not be revealed to the author. They can then report back to you with, and in, confidence. Some advisers are known to accept payment in kind. A selection of your books is fairly common. Less common is a fine dinner or a crate of wine, but might be more appreciated.

SEEKING ADVICE FROM COLLEAGUES

Sometimes it is not only advisable but crucial to discuss a proposal with a colleague or team of colleagues. Collaboration with marketing and production colleagues is an essential part of work for editors in educational publishing, for example, where content, layout and price combine absolutely in the drive for the right product for the market-place. No editor can make decisions on his or her own in this kind of publishing.

In consumer books publishing the decision to publish can be affected by considerations of marketing, pricing and publicity in which marketing colleagues will play a more important part than the editor. Sales and marketing may sometimes play the leading role in the decision to publish. In scholarly publishing, where content is considered absolute, even there the editor will probably seek the advice of colleagues in export marketing because overseas sales will make all the difference to the total sales of an academic monograph. Illustrated books of course are the prime example of editorial, rights and production working hand in glove, and if production and design are not involved from the earliest conceptual beginnings, costly mistakes are likely to ensue.

Any editor, whatever the list, should determine whose expertise is required on this project, in addition to his or her own, and enlist it from the word go.

ANALYSING THE INFORMATION GATHERED

Some weeks after an editor has first examined a book proposal (or more rarely, a typescript), and following on from discussions with colleagues and advisers, he or she will be in possession of a set of information and opinions, some of which constitute facts and others often masquerading as facts. If you are lucky, the collection of opinions and facts are as one and it is quite clear that you are dealing with a book that must be published: the focus is right, its length is right, the market is big enough (and can be reached), the price is what the market can bear and, furthermore, when all the copies to be printed have sold, you will make the profit desired by your publishing house. All criteria have been satisfied and a contract can be offered to the author. Reality of course is more a combination of positive and negative factors but the balance overall must be positive if you decide in favour of publication.

FACTORS INFLUENCING THE DECISION TO PUBLISH

Different editors and publishing houses will have different ideas about where their desired emphasis lies. Whatever the final motivation to publish – whether it is to keep an author who might go elsewhere if not signed up; or whether it is to add another title to a growing, vital list; or whether it is because it is a big revenue item that in business terms is vital to the finances of the company – there is one thing that unites all editors in this process. They must be absolutely satisfied that the print run is sustainable (i.e. that it is possible to sell that number of copies) and that when sold, the desired gross profit will be achieved.

This is the real bottom line for editors and if they sign up books that will not fit these absolutely basic criteria, they are being cavalier with their companies' investment. Every editor must be able to justify his or her actions. Those who are not able or willing to do that, must then accept the consequence of taking unnecessary risks and that includes losing the trust and faith of colleagues. Editors who effectively say, trust me, I know I'm right about this even though I can see doubts in everyone else's minds, will get little sympathy the next time they ask for someone else's commitment and support. Particularly tough on such editors are the sales force. It is very difficult for an editor who was very persuasive the first time around about a book that failed, to repeat the process at subsequent sales conferences. An editor is only as good as his or her last prediction.

Just as reprehensible is to 'fix the figures' – to add some sales here and there in order to raise the print run and produce a financial statement for the book that will make it look healthy. The chances are that you will be caught out by colleagues who have a good grasp of typical sales figures, whether in the home market or overseas, and you will be asked to revise your figures down. Even if you are lucky enough not to be caught out, if the sales are not there to be made, unsold stock will eventually manifest itself as yet another case of overprinting.

THE WRONG DECISION

That said, editors can be genuinely unfortunate. They will have done their homework and preparation in relation to both print run and profit only to discover that a competitor brings out a similar title at the same time or that public taste and interest change in the interval between signing the book up and publishing it. Your book fails for reasons strictly beyond your control.

Can an editor be properly brought to account for this? Possibly. Should an editor be so ignorant about what is going on in other publishing houses? Editors, authors and agents do talk to each other. It is not that difficult to pick up market intelligence. As for the matter of changing public taste, a book should not be so long in its gestation that it does stand the risk of arriving in the market-place just when the market moves on; editors must also be confident they are backing a trend and not a flash in the pan.

There are no easy solutions to this predicament except to emphasise strongly the importance of finding out what your competitors are up to as part of your market intelligence. And never confuse 'gimmick' books with trend books, however many your competitors are producing. Gimmick books work well enough but usually on a one-off basis. Also, band-wagons have an unpleasant tendency to roll to a halt.

WORKING WITH AGENTS

The great majority of consumer books authors have agents. Specialist authors seldom do. Agents, on average, recoup about 10 per cent of an author's earnings for the service they provide. For specialist authors the income they earn from their books is far too modest to justify using agents and an agent would simply not be interested in putting in the work they do for such a small return.

A good agent is valuable to author and publisher alike. A good agent knows how to get the best deal for the author but also respects the author's needs. A good deal will constitute not only the best financial package but also effective and well-planned marketing campaigns, successful subsidiary rights activity and a relationship with a publisher where the author feels wanted, noticed and taken care of. Sometimes an attractive financial package is on the table but the rest is lacking. It is up to the agent to try and get a good balance between all these things, although the final decision about which offers to accept lies with the author, who will on the whole take the agent's advice.

A good agent can also fight for an author when he or she is let down or inadequately treated by a publisher. Similarly, an agent will bring pressure to bear on an author when the author fails in his or her side of the bargain. An agent's job is to try to construct a situation that works for both parties.

When an agent is involved, the editor will have to deal with the author via the agent. It is perfectly possible, indeed essential, to develop a relationship directly with the author provided that, clearly, you are not trying to squeeze the agent out or playing author against agent, which is not acceptable.

Agents also expect to be fully informed about a book's progress, to have their enquiries dealt with promptly and to see that promises are carried out. They keep editors on their toes but the best ones keep their authors on their tocs too. An agent can be an invaluable ally when an author proves to be difficult to work with.

THE INCREASING POWER OF AGENTS

Agents used to be criticised sometimes for not taking sufficient interest in the detail of the book and only being concerned with financial issues. The situation has changed and agents have become powerful. This has happened for the following reasons:

- Sub-rights have assumed an even greater importance in the publishing equation. There are valuable rights to be sold in serialisation, film and broadcasting, and electronic publishing, as well as the traditional area of translations and co-publications. Gradually agents have felt less inclined to sell sub-rights in a book because they believe they have the expertise and connections to retain and sell on rights just as successfully as, and sometimes more so than, the rights departments of publishing houses. By retaining sub-rights, the income that comes to the author, and therefore to themselves, will be greater as the publisher will not be extracting their share of earnings. Few authors will quarrel with such a position. In reality, however, the question is whether the agents are more successful than the publishers in selling rights. It is difficult to get hold of data that will prove the case, but the assumption is growing, making the position of the publisher far less secure than it used to be.
- Agents have also acted on another perceived trend, which is that the true editorial role within publishing houses is diminishing. Evidence, yet again, is anecdotal but there is a broad and growing perception that editors are under too much pressure to spend time on the kind of detail required to publish a book and an author fully. Agents now involve themselves with manuscript development to a greater degree than perhaps was common before. Some of the functions of an editor

have begun to cross over to the agent. From the point of view of the publisher this is not a good development as the relationship between the author and the in-house editor is intrinsic to successful publication. This development is likely to continue until senior publishing management takes a long hard look at editorial workloads, and while experienced editors convert to becoming agents, as a number have in the past five years. Such experience within an agency is of course highly attractive to authors.

• Successful authors, and especially consumer authors, have become very powerful. These are commodities that every publishing house wants, and is sometimes able to pay for. As publishing becomes more conspicuously commercial, so will the authors. Agents are strong allies championing the rights and needs of their authors. Rights and needs are now beginning to encompass such issues as copy-editing of manuscripts, marketing treatments and jacket design, with the author, through an agent, making clear his or her demands.

GUIDELINES ON WORKING WITH AGENTS

It is difficult for a young or inexperienced editor to establish credibility with agents. Clearly an agent prefers to deal with editors who have a track record, although there are a few who, wisely, see young editors as the future of the industry and actively encourage them.

1 Be prepared to make frequent contact with agents. Go and see them; don't expect them to come to you.
2 Take them to lunch so you can talk about what you are looking for in a relaxed social setting. Some agents welcome visits to their offices by young editors.
3 To begin with, and to get the measure of you, they will probably offer their least likely candidates for publication, to see what you make of them. Reject them with care. This is a good way of demonstrating your grasp of content and market. It could impress and lead to better things.
4 Study their author lists carefully. Make sure you know which agent handles which author. The agent will expect you to have done your homework.
5 Suggest ideas for authors they handle. They will like your ingenuity and enterprise (but only if the ideas are good ones). If they 'steal' your ideas and hand them to another publisher, avoid them. This is a tough and upsetting thing to happen, but it's unavoidable if you are dealing with anyone less than scrupulous. Being in frequent contact is probably the best way to avoid this happening because you are constantly reminding them of your ownership of the idea.

6 To begin with, you cannot hope to deal with the really big names in agency work – some of whom it seems have become more famous than their authors. Unless you have (a) the nerve, (b) the ingenuity to come up with a truly original publishing idea and (c) the enterprise to get through to them directly, you are not likely to encounter them until you have a track record and have become a more interesting prospect as far as they are concerned. By then you will have acquired the experience needed to deal with their tough bargaining style.

An excellent book on agents and their work is Carole Blake's *From Pitch to Publication.*

INTUITION VERSUS FACTS

To draw this section on evaluation to a close, think about the difficult question of intuition versus facts. One of the infuriating things about books and publishing is that just as you appear to have formulae and models nicely sewn up, something comes along that disproves them and the market behaves in wholly unanticipated ways. These are books that did not conform but worked, and worked well.

Coming across a wonderful book which does not meet the usual desiderata is rather like seeing beauty or knowing truth. It is undeniable and it is, thank heavens, a rare experience. Supporting such books before the world has recognised them for the masterpieces they are can be a stressful although ultimately liberating experience for the editor. It is stressful because of the constant pressure to prove to the world you are right. If you are right, the confidence that flows from that is very exciting and can mark real growth. It can turn an editor from just a good, competent, workaday person into somebody quite special.

Such books are rare and the editor to match them has to have a good command of the content or the message so that he or she can convey it to colleagues and the market with enormous conviction. Exceptional books need exceptional foresight and commitment and if you discover you have that, even seemingly fleetingly, rejoice. You may have talent.

FACTORS THAT CAN LEAD TO BAD DECISIONS

The inexperienced editor can count on two things. First, there are rules and guidelines to follow, and secondly that there will be older, more experienced colleagues around who can advise when the going gets rough. However, your senior colleagues are likely to be pretty busy too and can't keep a constant eye on you. In this section the most common areas of trouble are touched on.

BEING COMPROMISED

Being compromised means 'getting too close for comfort'. This can happen at any time but is especially common when young editors are starting out and are rather anxious to be seen signing up books. They receive what looks like a rather interesting proposal from a hopeful author, express unqualified enthusiasm and very quickly the author is convinced that he or she is definitely going to be offered a contract. When the editor remembers with a start that he or she has to propose the book formally to colleagues, this can lead to embarrassment at the very least and resentment at worst on the part of the author. The process of formal commitment often entails, don't forget, a reader's report, and if that reader's report is negative then both author and editor are going to be doubly discomforted.

The editor can also be compromised in other areas. Promises are made about promotion campaigns, jacket designs, and so on; authors ask for and are assured expensive author tours because in effect the editor felt too close to say 'no'. This kind of treatment, based on weakness, can lead to resentment and anger amongst other colleagues because the company is being asked to foot the bill for an editor's inability to remain on a professional footing with the author.

All editors have rather embarrassing stories about giving in to authors' demands which actually undermined those editors' professionalism. They have almost inevitably come about because the editor becomes too friendly with the author. There is nothing intrinsically wrong with being a friend to your authors. Just always remember that some of them have very good reason to want to be friends with you. It's always best to establish initially a strong and mutually respectful relationship with your author (perhaps spread over the publication of several books) before allowing the relationship to move from the sociable to the social.

Remember that until you have got to the point where a book has been approved and you are now able to issue a contract, when talking to the author always use the words, 'If we go ahead with publication . . .'.

GETTING TOO CLOSE TO THE SUBJECT

It is just as well to maintain some distance between yourself and your subject. A dash of objectivity is a good thing. Being in love with philosophy can be the source of enormous energy and commitment if your job is to be the philosophy editor. However, if you steep yourself in the subject, you can take your involvement to the point where all philosophical writing is simply regarded as wonderfully interesting and worthwhile. Good reasons can be found for publishing everything except the truly diabolical. You are now a commercial risk. Remind yourself that you can read these worthwhile manuscripts for nothing but, if turned into books, how keen would people be to spend money on them?

In the *Introduction* the recruitment of editors from relevant professional spheres – specifically academics, teachers and lawyers – was mentioned. This problem of being too close to the subject to be commercially critical is a particularly pertinent one for them.

MISJUDGING DATA

The process of collecting data to support a publishing proposal was mentioned earlier. Part of that data might involve providing statistical evidence of market size. Even when the evidence suggests a large potential market, never forget that the book has to meet the needs of that large market. Remainder bookshops are rather instructive places to visit for evidence of this: they are testimony to the sloppy thinking of publishers who thought that any book on a subject that is known to be popular would sell. Book buyers are in fact rather more discriminating than that. A book must be seen to be serving a purpose, or to have some exceptional characteristics, even in a large market.

At the other extreme, discovering through statistics that your market is very small could cause you to turn down a book whose real potential is far wider. There is the example of an editor who was offered her first art therapy book (an edited collection) some years ago. Because she knew nothing about the area, she set about finding out how many art therapists there were in Britain. She discovered there were just 250 – hardly enough to constitute a real market. However, she was fortunate because the book's editor was a persuasive and articulate woman who persisted in educating her about art therapy and about the far wider audience that existed for the book in the fields of social work, medicine and psychiatry. She took the risk (and was lucky to have colleagues prepared to share the risk) and when the book was published, discovered that they were publishing to an extremely enthusiastic and not so small market. These book buyers (made up of art therapists, nurses, psychiatrists and psychotherapists) were not only very keen to buy really good books in their field, but were up to date on who was writing what, when the publications were going to appear, and so on. That book and others from the same team of writers were a great success, but it would not have happened if the editor had insisted on taking the statistics on art therapy at face value.

BAD TIMING

Some editors enter a market too early, others too late. For example, an editor by luck or prescience may be attracted to a title that is rather ahead of itself. If the market is not ready, the sales will not be made. When the books of Michel Foucault first appeared in English, they sold only a couple of hundred copies a year. It usually takes some nerve and conviction to stick with such titles when the accountants want them remaindered or pulped. In this case, the editor struck luck: the combination of intuition and a kindly management for whom the editor worked succeeded because eventually Foucault's work was recognised and sales rocketed. However, if you find yourself in a seemingly similar situation and your intuition is proved wrong, you will not be allowed the same chance again. You must be convinced by a new book or list when you are the first to enter a new field.

COPY-CAT PUBLISHING

It takes less flair to enter a field that is transparently a large one where many publishers are active. You are simply following the crowd. But that again does not necessarily pay off. Always remember that today's publishing programmes represent publishing decisions that may have been made as much as five years ago. By now, those publishers will have discovered through the evidence of their own sales, that the market is contracting. By the time your book comes on stream, the party is over.

There is only one way to avoid this: if you must copy another publisher, do your homework. Never take the books and the market for granted.

UNDERSTANDING AND REMEMBERING YOUR OBJECTIVES

Always have a clear understanding, from management, of how many titles a year you are expected to acquire and/or the revenue targets you are meant to achieve. In conjunction with both, remember to judge the amount of time and effort you can devote to each individual title on offer. It is very easy to devote too much of both to individual titles when you should be spreading resources more evenly. This is of course perfectly appropriate when the title is going to be a high-revenue earner, but too often even experienced editors will allow themselves to be distracted by work on titles that are not exceptional in this respect. Remember, too, that your marketing colleagues also do not have endless amounts of time or resources to devote to individual titles, except those extra special ones. Everyone, including you, is engaged in the same difficult game of trying to spread time, effort and other resources in the most effective way.

CASE STUDIES

1   A large international publishing company published two books by an
    author who first came to public attention through his contributions to
    radio. He was a brilliant observer of foreign countries, who was able
    to bring a sometimes unconventional but acute gaze to what he saw
    around him. His first two books sold in the hundreds of thousands. A
    third book was proposed in which the author would observe and
    comment on a country out of his habitual milieu. Furthermore, there
    would be a TV series tie-in. The publishers signed up the book with
    enthusiasm, given his track record. As time went on, the progress of
    the book stumbled as the author became more and more involved in
    the TV programme. The author's agent was not as 'visible' as one
    might have expected. The book was late arriving. The publishers were
    not able to put the full amount of effort that they would have wished
    into pre-publication activities because they needed the book to coin-
    cide with the TV programme. Everything was done in a rush. When
    the book came out, its sales just about got into five figures, effectively
    a failure in this kind of publishing. A large advance had been paid.

QUESTION

It is highly unlikely that any publisher or editor would not have signed
up the book, given the author's track record. With the benefit of hindsight, which is a gift available to all of us, what do you think went
wrong and why? At what point do you think your confidence might
have started to wobble, and what would you have done?

2   A literary editor was presented with the fourth novel by a young writer
    yet to make his mark. The first two had been published by a highly
    reputable but small publisher, the third by a similar house. The sales
    had been fairly abysmal. Yet the reviews had been warm and he was
    always described as 'promising'. On completion of his fourth novel, the
    literary agent acting on his behalf sent it to his second publisher, who
    read it, said he did not like it, and turned it down. The agent then sent
    it to a number of publishers. Our editor in question did like it and
    presented it to his colleagues. He really had to struggle to get it
    accepted. He was allowed to contract it, but did rather worry about it,
    given that he had not had enthusiastic backing from his colleagues

and the author's previous books had failed. In the event, the book was published to rave reviews and to massive sales. Most of us will probably have read that book and laughed ourselves silly, it was that good.

QUESTION

If you had been in our editor's position, what do you think would have motivated you so strongly to commit to the novel? What arguments would you have used to try to persuade your colleagues? What steps might you have taken to ensure that the book was a success? Would you have stuck your neck out in a situation like this, and why?

Committing projects for publication

3

In this chapter we shall be covering the following issues:

- presenting submissions for contract approval
- profit and loss accounts
- production costs
- aiming for accuracy in length and delivery
- contracts
- rights
- creating the basis for good author/editor relationships

As should be evident by now, it is foolish for any editor to think that he or she can galvanise a whole team of publishing colleagues behind a book without doing the things that are necessary to obtain their willing commitment. You can ask for their commitment and get a formal agreement but what is far more effective is to have properly persuaded your colleagues of the rightness of your decision to publish a particular book. Not all publishing houses – especially small ones – go through a formal process of gaining approval for a book before issuing a contract to the author. Indeed, even those who have some sort of approval process do not necessarily require of the editor that he or she provides a written submission justifying a book's publication.

Written submissions are required in most specialist publishing, and consumer books publishers, if not needing a report from an editor, will demand detailed costings and profit and loss figures, including figures on possible earnings from subsidiary rights. Consumer books publishers will also require that the editor submit a detailed marketing plan or campaign which might be crucial to their ability to sell that book successfully. Some of the large corporations have systems where books are approved at two levels: first at middle management level, before being referred up to a committee made up of the most senior managers in the house.

THE WRITTEN SUBMISSION

If your house requires a written submission, the first time you write one you will inevitably feel nervous; some people will deal with their anxiety by claiming that such a written procedure is nothing less than a chore, a strait-jacket even. The process of writing something down, however, can be rather valuable. Marshalling a set of arguments to justify a book's publication represents your first real attempt to market that book. It is the first time you can begin to specify what the book is about – in essential terms – and what it is about those essential characteristics that adds up to something that people will want to buy. What does it have over other books? What is it about the author that is special? Is there something extraordinarily timely about the subject matter? Does it fit in with the house's publishing plans?

You are now drawing up a list of selling points. If you can't do that for a book, then ask yourself why it should be published. If you haven't yet encountered the experience of flaying around for a good set of reasons for publishing a book, then you are either highly inventive or just plain lucky so far. Experienced editors will admit that there have been times when they did find it a little difficult to explain why they were proposing publication. Some of the reasons why they found themselves in this strange position are dealt with in the section below. More often than not, however, the difficulty arises because the book itself is unfocused, or it has very little that is exceptional about it. It will be one of those books that, when published, will be damned by the reviewers as a 'useful book', easily forgotten and contributing not a lot to your revenues.

There is another reason why editors sometimes cannot analyse a book's strengths – they are simply not good editors because they cannot classify their products; they cannot ultimately distinguish one from another – all are just books. Such editors are not likely to grow and develop successfully in the long run because they lack the ability properly to understand their product and the market for it.

The written submission, then, is a careful set of arguments that will be supported by various pieces of evidence. If it is a specialist book, part of the evidence will be reports from expert advisers. These should be reasonably detailed – one paragraph will not do. An adviser is expected to comment on the value of the content, the readership and the competition, and, by the nature of these things, such a report is likely to run to at least two pages. Many specialist houses have questionnaires that they have developed over the years to ask precisely the sorts of questions that the house will find most valuable when answered with care. On the other hand, all questionnaires are structured documents and some advisers prefer to evaluate a proposal in their own way. However your advisers work, you must know the fundamental questions that need to be answered.

EVALUATION CHECKLIST

- Who exactly are the readers? It could be a range of readers but they must be specified.
- Have you good evidence (sales figures) for the success of this kind of book?
- What course or training requirements will the book meet (if appropriate)?
- Is the book pitched at the right level to meet those needs?
- Do the proposed readers use books or expect to have to read them as part of their training and education (if appropriate)? For example, social workers recognise that they need to keep updating their knowledge base but are notoriously bad at reading because they haven't got the time.
- Is the book's presentation (layout and format) appropriate to what the reader needs or finds 'user friendly'?
- What are the competitive texts and what are this book's strengths and weaknesses by comparison? Are there any in preparation?
- Is pricing a strong consideration?
- How big is the market? What statistical evidence has the adviser (or you) got about comparable successful books?
- How do these readers normally buy books – through the shops, or college or education reps, or by direct mail?
- Is there sub-rights potential, including repurposing the material into other formats?
- If direct marketing is required, can appropriate lists be purchased (if not available in house)?
- Is there a possibility of making a special sale to a related organisation or institution? This would mean selling them bulk copies at special discounts. The discounts will almost inevitably be less than trade discounts so this could add up to a good 'deal'.
- Are there obvious omissions in content, or should material be removed?
- Are sample chapters required?

PROFIT AND LOSS ACCOUNT

If you have satisfied yourself that the book should be recommended for publication, you will also need to show your colleagues that it is going to be financially viable.

Drawing up a profit and loss account for a new book is therefore an essential part of the process of contracting books, whether specialist or consumer. Profit and loss accounts differ from one publisher to another. For example, an academic profit and loss account will normally be taken to the gross profit level. It deals only with production and royalty costs, and sales.

Consumer books publishers are just as vitally interested in their marketing and promotion costs, because their sales campaigns are a large and expensive part of the publication of a book, and such publishers need to have a good understanding of just how much it is going to cost them to sell a book. Although by and large a consumer book will have a marketing and promotion budget set for it, it is not unknown for some of them to have been launched on the back of campaigns that turned out to be so ambitious that the costs ate catastrophically into otherwise decent revenues.

In specialist publishing, these variable costs are much more predictable and tend to be absorbed into the general overhead costs of the house. Unlike trade publishers, these publishers are not working in an elastic market that might expand if one throws a huge promotion campaign at it. Specialist markets are relatively inelastic and therefore publishers serving them have fairly well-defined ideas, based on experience, about what percentage of a book's revenue should be spent on its marketing and promotion.

Examples of profit and loss accounts for specialist and consumer books are shown below. Whether working to a gross or a net profit, what each publisher is seeking to achieve is a degree of profitability on each book that ensures that, taken together with the performance of other books on the list, the financial results enable the publishing house to carry on trading healthily. Just as other things vary, so does that desired level of profitability from one sector of publishing to another. Consumer books publishers can live on lower levels than specialist publishers because their books sell faster and realise their potential revenues sooner than specialist ones. Specialist books, because they are slower to sell and sit in the warehouse longer, require a higher degree of profitability on each copy sold because it takes longer to recoup the investment and those storage costs have to be paid for.

The profit and loss accounts shown below are inevitably simplified versions of the documents that normally pass over our desks. For example, they omit a line for returns. But in some sectors of publishing, returns rates are so high that they are budgeted for in the profit and loss account. Many companies have a good understanding of what their average returns rate is in any given year and if it is on the high side, they will enter it as a cost to be deducted from the gross profit. This is a very wise precaution to take because what looks like a good initial sales performance for a book (the reps having done a good job selling it in), can turn into failure when those books, whose production costs you have paid for, make their way back into the warehouse.

PROFIT AND LOSS ACCOUNT FOR A CONSUMER TITLE

The following is a P & L for a title that would have failed if it had relied solely on trade sales in the home market:

Price: £15.95	
Home sales	£14,391 (1,800 copies)
Export sales	£3,454 (675 copies)
Specials	£34,800 (book club deal and US co-publication)
Total sales	£52,645
Production costs	£29,510
Cost of frees	£643
Royalties	£5,984
Total costs	£36,137
Trading profit	£16,508 (31.4%)
Add rights income	£7,500
Gross profit	£24,008 (46%)

INFLUENCE OF SUBSIDIARY RIGHTS INCOME ON PROFITABILITY

Quite clearly this consumer book would not have made it if it had relied on sales through bookshops alone. It has succeeded through several crucial additions. The first is 'specials', in this case 6,000 copies sold to a book club and a further 3,000 copies to an American co-publisher. There is also additional rights income. In this case, an advance on an Italian translation which is netting £2,500 to the publisher and an advance of £5,000 for a paperback edition, which another publisher is putting up. Overall, the performance in percentage terms is only 46 per cent but the publisher decided that although the ideal gross profit should be 50 per cent, the result was good enough to proceed. The publisher took the view that the title was a good enough 'filler' for the list – a title whose performance is not particularly distinguished in financial terms but has merit in others, including keeping up one's publishing targets for a list and trading with other publishers.

What has actually swung the balance in favour of this title is the subsidiary rights earnings because without it, the book's gross profit would only have been 31 per cent. This is why subsidiary rights managers in trade publishing houses are extremely important people who know exactly how to milk the last drop of income out of a book. It is not that unusual, as in the case above, for the subsidiary rights income actually to make the difference between scraping by and achieving an acceptable profit.

PRODUCTION COST IMPLICATIONS

When costings for this book were originally done, a print run of 3,000 copies was envisaged. As we know, the book sold many more copies than that because of a book club deal and a sale to an American publisher. What made the book highly problematic was the production costs. The author exceeded the agreed number of illustrations, although the editor felt that these extra illustrations were merited and did not ask the author to cut them. The net effect, however, was that the illustrations and the fees associated with them constituted over 23 per cent of the entire production costs. This reveals how illustrated books only make financial sense when they are high print-run books where economies of scale can justify this substantial element in the production costs.

The much-needed book club and US sales were able to bring relief not only to the sales revenue but also by spreading the plant costs over a far bigger print run. Without both, this book would have been hopelessly costly and unprofitable. The extra sales were also made in areas where very high discounts operate: book clubs and co-publications. If publishers relied heavily on these kinds of book, they would be struggling financially.

An extended case study featuring a P & L for a specialist book that went horribly wrong is featured at the end of this chapter.

ACCURACY IN LENGTH AND DELIVERY

However speculative the content of a book is likely to be, there are two factual elements that you must nail: delivery date and length. The editor and author inevitably discuss this together and must agree on both. At least, they do at the very beginning but somewhere along the line, the 'facts' can change.

Both these issues will be tackled in the course of reviewing a proposal for publication. But they appear in this section on 'commitment' because both of them constitute a contractual commitment.

Getting the author to deliver to time and length is one of the most notorious problems that editors encounter. This is especially so in specialist publishing where the authors tend not to write for a living. Full-time writers who are dependent on their writing for income are far more disciplined about both, for reasons that are obvious.

LENGTH

On balance, length presents less of a problem to the editor than the delivery date. Most authors have a fairly good idea of how many words they need to do justice to a topic. Every now and then, you do come across an author who seems to be shooting for a target that is on the low side.

Too short?

You need to consider:

1 Whether the proposed length is simply not enough to go into the kind of detail that the author has outlined in the proposal. Experience built up over time will help the editor to be a good judge of such matters, but, for example, if an author is proposing to write 40,000 words on a topic that you know tends to be covered in no less than 60,000, you must question this.
2 Do the economics of this particular short book really make sense? Publications of less than 100 pages cannot really be priced up. Therefore, if the price is going to be low, the question is whether you can sell this publication in sufficient quantities to justify the marketing costs that it will inevitably have to carry. There are basic costs such as review copies, warehousing and repping that simply cannot be avoided.
3 Another question, which is likely to be raised by the sales staff, is, does it have a spine? If it's very short, and effectively does not have a spine, it won't be seen amongst the other books on the shelves. Where in the bookshop is it going to be stocked? Booksellers are not well disposed to book products that cannot be put on the shelves, which is something the editor must consider.

Too long?

You are less likely to encounter an author wanting to write under length than over length. Writing concisely is an art and one that is gradually dying out. Someone has yet to explain why so many authors seem to feel they need more and more space to say what they want to say. In specialist publishing, books are increasingly put together by a number of contributors – the edited collection. These collections inevitably go over length when perhaps ten or more people jointly compound the problem of writing to target.

An author who proposes to write a book that is way above average length must be tackled from the moment the proposal is under scrutiny.

1 The extra length will add to all the production costs incurred and you may not be able to compensate for the extra costs by charging a higher price. Most experienced publishers know at any time what the 'going rate' is for a particular type of book in a market and anything that deviates from that model should be taken seriously. The unit cost of the book must lie in a healthy relationship to the price. If it is too high in relation to the price, the book will have lower profits. To put it another way, you cannot incur Rolls Royce production costs if you want to sell a car at family budget prices. High production costs can be compensated for when you can confidently set a high print run – when you are certain that a large number of copies will sell – because in this situation, economies of scale are achievable.

2 *Never* make the mistake of printing more copies of a book in order to get the unit cost down. This solecism is something of an old chestnut in publishing, and yet it is still possible to find people who feel moved to commit it. It is a terrific risk to take, and the unsold copies more often than not will fill the shelves of remainder bookshops. In many publishing houses, of course, it is sales and marketing who either take responsibility for setting the print run and price, or do it jointly with editorial, thereby ensuring that some healthy realism is brought into the process.

3 Another consequence of writing over length is that the editor may be forced to publish a book in a format that would not have been his or her first choice. In specialist publishing, where there are relatively inelastic markets, what an editor foresaw as a paperback could emerge as a hardback because the length would lead to a paperback price that the market could not bear. This is a highly effective point to make to an author if you do disagree over length.

DELIVERY

Delivery is more of a problem in practice than length. It is one thing to agree dates, and another to see the typescript arrive on time. Again, authors who write for their living are more likely to be reliable. A full-time academic, shall we say, who gets a regular salary is not likely to be under this sort of pressure. Neither is a professional, perhaps a lawyer, who can earn more in a week than he or she does from a year's royalties. Not delivering on time, usually referred to as 'slippage', is one of publishing's most difficult problems and is dealt with in greater depth in the following chapter.

These are some of the issues that need to be explored:

1 A new author will sometimes, because he or she wants to please the editor, propose a delivery date which is unrealistically optimistic. This frequently happens in the case of edited collections where the volume's (external) editor has simply underestimated the time taken to gather all the contributions in and then lick them into good shape. He or she has not realised that at least two of their contributors will inevitably let them down and deliver their chapters months later than everyone else.

2 The most sensible thing from the outset is to anticipate such dilemmas and to talk the author or editor through the situation, whether this is a single, joint- or multi-authored book. You should certainly do so in the case of joint authorship where each author may have differing ideas on how long it is going to take to write the book, and the difference has been neither properly aired nor resolved.

3 You will need to find out if the author has any extra teaching or research commitments coming up in the next year, or indeed, other writing commitments which might affect the ability to deliver on time.

4 You also need to know if the author will be travelling overseas for any lengthy periods of time, which might also affect his or her writing schedule.

5 There might be personal circumstances that could affect the author's ability to finish on time, such as changing jobs, or moving house. You cannot, of course, plan for Fate or acts of God intervening! You can do something, however, to anticipate more mundane events that will be taking place.

6 If an author has not written a book before, you need to explore whether he or she really understands what is involved.

Ask the author how he or she plans to go about the writing. During this conversation, reality will slowly emerge and you are more likely to come up with a delivery date that can be kept than one that is hopelessly unrealistic.

Whatever is decided regarding length and delivery date, it is vital that the editor conveys to the writer that neither is a moveable feast. These are real facts as far as you are concerned, and contractually so, and they are part and parcel of your forward publishing programme. The writer needs to understand that deviation from them is a very serious professional issue for you, the editor. However friendly your early conversations are with your new author, it is well worth getting serious with him or her about this. If you do, you are less likely to experience nasty surprises further down the line.

THE CONTRACT

Once everything has been agreed, the contract must be sent as soon as possible to the author. Any author is likely to get frustrated if the contract takes weeks to arrive. A contract should be sent to an author no more than a month after the deal has been agreed and the advance should follow on very rapidly after the document has been signed. Just as an editor would be remiss to send an author a contract for a book without going through the full business of approval from colleagues in the house, he or she is equally remiss to lose momentum over the paperwork after having gone through the effort of examining and accepting the proposal. Paperwork is important. The author wants commitment and as far as the author is concerned, nothing substitutes for a contract. For high-profile consumer books authors, a contract should be in their hands within days, of course.

VARIATIONS IN CONTRACTS

Contracts vary, certainly from sector to sector, and from publisher to publisher. However, in any particular sector, the contracts of the most prominent houses tend to look rather similar. No publisher really dares to get badly out of line with the norm. In the past publishers and authors were a little more discreet about the terms and conditions they were setting or receiving. Today contracts and the terms and conditions under which authors are handled are that much more public; people do not feel that they should be secretive about these things.

On the other hand, it is worth mentioning that the norm can certainly vary from country to country. Option clauses are quite common in North American specialist publishing contracts but not in British ones. Both American and British consumer books publishers are likely to have option clauses in their contracts. Option clauses state that the author is obliged to offer the publisher his or her next book. Unless an author has signed up for a specific two- or three-books deal, an agent is likely to take the view that the option clause is a restrictive practice. So do many authors, including specialist ones, and if they are not satisfied with their publisher, they will find ingenious ways of getting around the option clause when they write their next book. On the other side, the publishers will take the view that having made the commitment to, and taken the risk with, the author's previous book, they are entitled to 'enjoy' the benefits of success that might come with the next title. If the previous title was not very successful, then perhaps the publisher will not feel too proprietorial! There are arguments on both sides, but perhaps option clauses are now rather anachronistic in a world where freedom of choice is part of the *Zeitgeist*.

The elements of a contract which are most likely to vary between sectors are advances, royalties and the subsidiary rights terms. For example, if you ask consumer books publishers what an 'average' advance might be for a decent but not exceptional (in commercial terms) book, the sum of £5,000 or more (and sometimes, much, much more) might very well be mentioned. Ask an academic publisher and that average advance is likely to be more in the region of £1,500. Some scientific publishers offer no advances at all. All reflect the elasticity of the respective markets as well as the custom of their particular sector of publishing.

Huge advances and royalty earnings are almost entirely the province of consumer publishing, although they are not entirely unknown in specialist publishing either. There is a famous author of an equally famous textbook in economics who is said to have bought and to run a private aircraft with the proceeds of his royalties. He is very much the exception. The issue of very large advances does exercise many in consumer publishing because of the consequences that flow from unearned advances. Granted, there is considerable income to be earned from co-publications, translations, and notably, serialisations, which can help put book revenue on a healthy footing, but essentially, when very large advances come into play, there is really only one issue here: securing an author at a high price even if projected royalty earnings for the author do not cover the size of the advance.

This is an issue for the boardroom. It is highly unlikely that anybody less than the most senior publishing managers in the house will be involved in such a decision, for it is an investment decision that goes beyond the normal parameters of 'investing in authors'. In these circumstances, the author has become a valuable commodity, to be bought and sold for the highest price.

ROYALTIES

Royalties vary between sectors but not greatly between houses in a given sector. Most publishers bunch around the norm in their particular part of the industry. *Escalator clauses* that allow an author's royalty to rise with sales are more common in consumer than specialist publishing because of the need to reward a popular author for exceptional sales. Authors' agents are likely to demand such escalator clauses for their clients. One efficient way of dealing with the burden of increasing royalties is to try to tie in the timing of a reprint with the next step up in royalties. Reprinting is a more profitable business than creating a book from scratch because so many costs – origination costs – are amortised at reprint stage. Therefore, the book is now able to absorb more comfortably the increased cost of higher royalties.

However you have calculated the advance, royalties or subsidiary rights terms, the complete package for the author has to reflect what the real revenue-earning capacity of the book is likely to be. At the very least, you must expect that the advance will have been earned on the sale of the very first print run. The profit and loss account for the book shows what the royalty earnings will be on the first print run. Any advance that exceeds it can only be justified by exceptional subsidiary rights income or serial rights income, or reprint potential. If you are confident that a title will remain in print for many years and that you will be reprinting stock on a regular basis, then a higher advance may be perfectly acceptable.

There are several additional points to be made about contracts:

1 The editor really must check every element in them before getting them signed. Not all publishing houses have dedicated contracts departments. In some houses, drawing up a contract is now included in the editor's brief and quite often the editor will assign this task to his or her assistant. However bright and willing this person is, he or she is comparatively inexperienced. It is vital that the editor check that the contract is correct. In large consumer houses, the presence of a contracts department is the norm. With large earnings and payments at stake, getting the contract right is paramount.

2 Be reasonable over subsidiary rights earnings. Authors are the lifeblood of publishing and editors should be fair with them. Many international publishing conglomerates with offices on either side of the Atlantic sell stock to each other at something just above cost and then give the author perhaps 10 per cent of that income. For many books, where sales are likely to be only several hundred copies, or less, this low sum may be appropriate. The author is lucky to have the book distributed there at all. However, if you know that the book is going to sell perhaps several thousands of copies, provision should be made for a royalty on the actual receipts *in* the American market to be paid to the author. The bright authors will figure out this kind of deal for themselves, and ask for it. And even if they have not and an agent is involved, the agent certainly will.

3 Do not assume that your author has either read or understood the contract thoroughly. Many simply check the clauses relating to length, delivery, advances and royalties and sign it. Make a point of asking the author to examine the contract properly and to take you through questions about anything he or she does not understand. It is far better to clarify all legal matters with the author from the outset.

RIGHTS

Traditionally, publishers acquired volume and subsidiary rights that allowed them a high degree of exploitation. They could either exploit those rights themselves or they could sub-license them to another publisher. The sub-licensing of paperback, translation, co-edition and book club rights has been the most common area of activity for the rights departments of publishing houses. Other sub-rights that a publisher had expected to acquire within the contract were many and various and could include serial, anthology, periodical, broadcasting, film and repro-duction rights.

Gradually these powers have been eroded by direct challenge or by changes in practice that accept the inevitable. It is increasingly becoming the norm, for example, for literary agents to retain, on behalf of the author, rights in translations, in American editions, first serialisation, and dramatic, broadcasting and film performance. Where merchandising is also likely to provide significant income for the author, the agent will withhold those rights. In these instances, the agent will handle the rights directly on the assumption that more sub-rights income will flow in the direction of the author because the publishers will not be able to extract their 'cut'. Equally of relevance, as far as the author and agent are concerned, is that by excluding these rights from the contract, the agent will perhaps act more in the interests of the author than their publisher might when securing deals. The agent might also take the view that he or she has better connections for making deals than the publisher has. Clearly, these are the kinds of issue that are open to debate.

The swift development of digital technology, and its consequences for electronic rights, is a very tricky area. For example, if you produce an e-book, based on the original print version, is this another form of licensing or is the publisher simply delivering content in another form? There are many arguments over this. A literary agent would take the first point of view and the publisher the second. One thing we can be sure of is that if digital technology enables us to produce new forms of content delivery that are commercially successful, both the authors and their agents are less likely to hand over rights.

With all areas of rights, be sure of what you are buying, and if you are excluded from handling a particular sub-right, ask yourself if your paper product is likely to be damaged in the future by the existence of another form of content delivery.

Both subsidiary rights and the general area of contracts are complicated subjects that bear some proper attention from an editor. Two books, unparalleled for their breadth and excellence, are mandatory reading: Lynette Owen's *Selling Rights* and *Clark's Publishing Contracts* (also edited by Lynette Owen).

If you don't get to grips with this area, you could find yourself in the unhappy position of a large consumer publisher that negotiated a co-publication with an American publisher. The 3,000 copies they had produced for the American house, bearing its title page, logo, and jacket blurb, were roughly half-way across the Atlantic when it was discovered that they did not have the American rights to sell. This was certainly a very expensive mistake, but perhaps the embarrassment all round was worse. The publishers had to explain themselves not just to the American publishers but also to the author and the agent.

COMMON AREAS OF MISJUDGEMENT

MISJUDGING LENGTH

Getting the length wrong can change the dimensions of a book both materially and financially. If you have commissioned a book at 60,000 words with a print run of 5,000 copies and to sell at a price of £9.95, the revenue and costs will be documented in your budget. Anything that deviates from that on delivery is a deviation from your proposed budget, which is a serious issue. Unless, of course, you are able to revise your revenue up substantially.

For example, one editor commissioned a book at 60,000 words and was going to publish it in hardback at £25. This was a specialist book. When the hard copy and its disk arrived, the editor found she did have 60,000 words, but she also had 400 diagrams. The subject matter, as it happens, was one where diagrams integral to the text might well have been expected, and yet neither she nor the author had at any time discussed this; they had literally concentrated on the number of words needed and had forgotten that diagrams incur costs and need space too. In this case, the book changed from a planned, slim 150 pages to a weighty 350 pages and the price came out as £45. Sales were dramatically down on what had been originally envisaged because the price of the book had moved it out of the individual purchase market and into library sales only.

Although this sounds like an example of grotesque incompetence, it is not that rare. It is replicated in other ways. This is simply one example of someone failing to grasp, indeed to approach, the real dimensions of the book under contract. For consumer book publishers working in children's books or illustrated non-fiction, estimating accurately the number of illustrations and the different costs associated with line drawings, black-and-white and colour illustrations is clearly crucial.

MISJUDGING DELIVERY

This is probably the most common problem editors face in the whole area of keeping control of their editorial programmes. Slippage is a dirty word but one on everyone's lips when the annual budget round begins. This is such a tricky area that in the next chapter, it will be dealt with extensively. Suffice it to say for the moment that if a book is not available to be sold when one projected it would be, the revenue is not there to be earned and that is a financial let-down for the company. Preparing for delivery must begin the moment you sit down with the author to discuss a proposal. The author must be taken carefully through the context of the writing process. It signals to him or her that this part of the business is a very serious matter. The author must realise from the outset that meeting the delivery date is part of a bargain that has been struck. Explain to the author:

- That the book will be scheduled to appear on a publishing programme and that real dates have been assigned to it based on the delivery date that is in the contract.
- That these publishing programmes are not just delivery plans; they constitute financial projections for the house. Books that are delivered late unbalance the financial projections. This is a serious issue for both editors and authors who should be aware that the financial good health of a publishing house is desirable for good publishing.

If time is spent explaining to the author the broader planning and financial context of the house, and how his or her book fits into it, delivery is more likely to be taken seriously. The author will realise that he or she is not writing in isolation.

FIGHTING YOUR COLLEAGUES' JUDGEMENT

All editors should stop and think carefully when they find that the majority of their colleagues are not nearly as enthusiastic about a project as they are. It is all too easy when you have sweated over a proposal to dismiss the opinions of colleagues as ill-informed or unimaginative. They might be, but you would be very unusual indeed to be in a publishing house where everyone else except you is ill-informed or unimaginative.

Instead of concluding that the rest of the band is marching out of step, this is the time to reflect that maybe they can see something you can't. Maybe you have become so absorbed by the proposal, and by the author, that you cannot distance yourself from it and see it for what it is.

Who knows what the outcome of this hypothetical set of deliberations might be. The point is: get your colleagues on your side from the word go. Have very good reasons indeed for fighting them. It is a risky strategy. When the book comes on stream, there is a danger that they will remember it when they are producing or promoting or selling it as the book they did not quite believe in. This is not good for your book which, like all the others, needs all the help it can get in the publishing process. In reality, there is a balance to be struck between fighting your corner for books you truly believe in and reluctantly letting go of others.

The acid test in this situation is to ask yourself, 'If I had the money, would I pay for this book to be published and enter into a revenue-sharing deal with my house?' If you start to feel uneasy about the idea of investing that money, then think twice about sticking your neck out to get the book published.

GIVING AWAY LARGE ADVANCES

If there is one aspect of publishing which has been consistently reported in the media, it is the subject of large advances. To specialist publishers, this is not a central issue. Even if these publishers rarely pay five-figure advances, they may just as likely be guilty of paying larger advances than is wise or necessary. The basic ground rules are:

- Specialist publishers tend to have a rule of thumb that an advance should constitute between one third and one half of the total royalties to be earned on the first print run, or a sum that represents the total royalties earned in the first year. Pay more than that, and too much money is being put up front. The authors of specialist books usually have full-time jobs and salaries to go with them.
- This is not the case for consumer books authors who expect not just to be paid for their time writing but also well rewarded if they are writing best sellers. Calculation of the advance will very much depend on calculation of the print run, which will determine sales revenue,

plus revenue from subsidiary rights. Your figurework must be done carefully and provision for the author's advance will be a function not just of the proportion of the total royalty earning but also of competition from other publishers who might publish this author. If the author already publishes with you, you will consider the desirability of keeping him or her on your list, and what that might translate to in terms of advances.

These matters require careful thought and should only be taken on a case-by-case basis and in deliberation with colleagues when large sums of money are involved. Whichever way you determine a suitable advance, you must be able to provide sound evidence that the author will eventually earn it (even if it is when you get to the reprint), otherwise you are throwing your company's money away.

Also reflect that tempting though it is to offer large advances to desirable authors, quite often the author is actually rather more interested in other aspects of the publication deal. Some authors have stayed with houses that were not in a position to pay substantial advances because they were more interested in being part of a smaller house where they and their books could be given individual attention.

In the less glamorous world of specialist publishing, remember that authors are not really writing for income. They are primarily interested in prestige and recognition within their fields. For many of them, their concern will be with the reputation of the house, especially if it is strongly associated with excellence. If your house is building up its reputation, you would probably be better served bringing all your energies to bear on convincing the author of the quality of your list, with a marketing department to match it, than trying to entice him or her with larger than average advances.

Sadly, many editors have got themselves enmeshed with authors for whom advances are living proof of their personal worth. The editors have bowed to the pressure to give a higher advance, bent over backwards to persuade their colleagues that this is the right thing to do in order, first, to get the author and, second, to keep him or her on the list. In the fullness of time, when the author writes the next book, instead of remaining with the house, feeling appreciated, he or she scampers off to another one, and another one, in search of a perpetual royalty rainbow.

CASE STUDY

THE EDUCATION TEXTBOOK THAT WENT WRONG

A schoolbook textbook was commissioned in 1999, a year ahead of proposed syllabus changes. The publishers took a gamble on being first into the market, ahead of new editions of competitive texts.

Because there were no in-house resources to manage the design and production of the book, it was sent to an external packager. This was the first wrong decision. Less important and less costly books should have been sent to the packager at a time when resources were stretched. The wrong decision was compounded by an inadequate briefing of the pack- ager and several cost elements spiralled out of control. In addition, the page length was greatly over estimate and an excessive number of artworks were allowed.

When the book came out, it did not make the impact on the market that was expected, so when the book first reprinted, the print run was lower than had been anticipated. In fact there was great difficulty in achieving the minimum 60 per cent gross profit on the reprint that the publishers would at all times require. The publishers could not raise the price of the book because the market was so competitive.

Table 1a: Profit and loss forecast

	Year 1	Year 2	Year 3	Total
Price	£19.99	£19.99	£19.99	
Home sales	3,700	2,950	2,950	9,600
Home discount	20%	20%	20%	
Total sales	3,700	2,950	2,950	9,600
Revenue	£59,170	£47,176	£47,176	£153,523
Author's royalty (net receipts)	10%	10%	10%	
Royalty earned	£5,917	£4,718	£4,718	£15,352
Free copies (inspection copies)	300	50	50	
Total print run	4,000	3,000	3,000	10,000
Origination costs	£25,800	£400	£50	
Total manufacture	£15,000	£12,000	£12,000	
Total production	£40,800	£12,400	£12,050	£65,250
Unit cost	£10.20	£4.13	£4.02	£6.53
Gross profit	£12,453	£30,059	£30,409	£72,921
Gross profit %	21%	64%	64%	47%

Table 1b: Profit and loss actual

	Year 1	Year 2	Year 3	Total
Price	£19.99	£19.99	£19.99	
Home sales	3,600	1,950	2,950	8,500
Home discount	20%	20%	20%	
Total sales	3,600	1,950	2,950	8,500
Revenue	£57,571	£31,184	£47,176	£135,932
Author's royalty	10%	10%	10%	
(net receipts)				
Royalty earned	£5,757	£3,118	£4,718	£13,593
Free copies	400	50	50	
(inspection copies)				
Total print run	4,000	2,000	3,000	9,000
Origination costs	£46,002	£420	£12,574	
Total manufacture	£16,640	£9,802	£19,848	
Total production	£62,642	£10,222	£32,422	£105,286
Unit cost	£15.66	£5.11	£10.81	£11.70
Gross profit	£10,828	£17,844	£10,037	£17,053
Gross profit %	19%	57%	21%	13%

Table 2:   Comparison of costs

Costs	Estimated	Actual
Print run	4,000	4,000
Price	£19.99	£19.99
Extent	420 pp.	512 pp.
	£	£
Typesetting	4,200	3,500
Typesetting corrections	420	
Project management		4,000
Copy-editing	500	500
Proof-reading	400	400
Courier fees	100	200
Index preparation	200	325
Paste-up		6,120
Artwork drawing	7,000	14,290
Artwork corrections	900	420
Photo search fee	1,000	3,876
Photo reproduction fee	7,280	7,280
Colour origination	3,500	4,758
Cover origination	300	300
Cover material	34	34
Total origination	25,834	46,003
Print and bind	15,000	16,640
Total origination costs	40,834	62,643
Unit cost	10.21	15.66

In any case, the gamble did not pay off. The syllabus changes that the book was anticipating revealed that the book was bereft of a crucial topic common to all the examination boards. A revised edition had to be published the following year – with yet more pages, more artwork, more photos.

The bottom line is that the total sales over three years were 9,000 copies, revenue was £136,000 and the gross profit just £17,000.

To put this into perspective, the publishers would usually base their forecasts on gaining about 10 per cent of the market at the very least. Average candidate numbers for that subject were 30,000, so a 3,000 per annum reprint was an acceptable forecast. Publishers in this area tend to print more copies in the first year if there is a new course, because spending is higher and schools buy multiple sets of different texts.

A cautious three-year forecast for this book was to sell 10,000 copies, make revenue of £150,000 plus, and achieve a gross profit of £73,000. In fact, the sales were not that different from what was forecast, apart from the terrible dip in the second year, which nevertheless made an acceptable level of profit as the book was a straight reprint. Then more money had to be invested in the third year for the reasons given above.

Above are the profit and loss figures for the estimated and for the actual book, plus a line-by-line comparison of where the origination costs went beyond the publisher's estimates.

QUESTION

Where shall we start?

Here is a very good example of everything going wrong because of a lack of control. It is a vivid example of a profit and loss account bludgeoned by the effect of spiralling costs, compounded by less than adequate sales. It is also illustrative of issues raised in later chapters about timing of publications, researching your book and the market, prioritising resources, losing a grip on the true dimensions of the book, being trapped in a competitive situation, and being confident that you can deliver out of a very high investment a correspondingly high profit line.

From contract to delivery 4

In this chapter we are going to look at the following areas:

- the need for accuracy in progress chasing
- setting up a system for regular progress chasing
- 'safe' scheduling
- providing appropriate encouragement and support for the author
- planning ahead for delivery
- slippage
- failure to deliver
- dealing with unsatisfactory writing

This chapter covers the period between signature of the contract and the delivery date. It is a period often of benign neglect of the author on the part of the editor and, for the author, a crucial time partly spent wishing that the book did not exist (at least, as an idea) and partly spent writing furiously in order to complete it. Both parties tend to forget about each other. The editor is most likely to be reminded of the book and the author when asked to itemise the publishing programme for the year ahead, usually as part of the budgetary process.

THE NEED FOR ACCURACY IN PROGRESS CHASING

The author will be reminded of his or her part in the process when he or she receives a phone call, an email, or a letter asking if the book is going to plan. In many cases, that enquiry is arriving a little too late for the editor to keep control of the schedule. Budget time differs from publishing house to publishing house, depending on the financial year that the house follows, but it can be assumed that most budgets are put together at least six months before the start of the financial year. In effect, many editors can be writing serious letters of enquiry about the progress of a book six months before its expected arrival. This is simply too late.

Why does it happen? If editors only had to sign up one season's books and then wait for them to roll in, it probably would not happen. However, an editor's work is never done, as they say, for as soon as one book is signed up, the editor has to press on to another and another. Each new book proposal brings in ever-present new demands. Each new prospective author brings another set of problems, and pleasures of course. The process of examining and signing up new books is highly concentrated work, consuming both the editor's time and energy. It is actually quite difficult for editors to jump outside this process and when they have to, they often get quite irritable! Also, most editors fool themselves with the thought that the author is, of course, getting on with writing the book.

MIS- AND DISINFORMATION

Alas, many editors will be rudely awakened to the news that the author is going to be a month, three months, six months, sometimes a year later than planned, in delivering the finished manuscript. But even this news is not necessarily accurate news because some authors, frankly, lie about delivery and will offer a delay of one to three months simply to placate the editor. Others have badly misjudged how long it is taking them to do their writing and continue to be unable to gauge accurately how much more time they need to finish it. Those offering a delay of six to twelve months also have to be watched like hawks because, although some of them will eventually deliver, amongst these substantially late deliverers are authors who will never make it, for whom a book is either a fantasy or the beginnings of severe 'writing block' – often the two closely related. Such authors can be found in all sectors of publishing and it is very difficult to spot them as potential non-deliverers because their sincerity and their enthusiasm when they are contracted are as real as any other author's.

SLIPPAGE

Late delivery is known as *slippage* and is one of the worst sins that beset a publishing house. It messes up the whole system and is rather like introducing something fatal, such as legionnaires' disease, into the publishing programme. Slippage disrupts programmes and budgets, sours relations between author and editor, and between an editor and other staff; it tests patience and can create a climate of mistrust.

Slippage is a particular problem for specialist publishers whose authors are not full-time writers and for whom the gestation period for books is fairly lengthy, perhaps two years or more. It is of course not unknown in trade publishing – writer's block knows no boundaries. In 2003, BBC Radio 4 broadcast a programme on the late Douglas Adams, author of the phenomenally successful *Hitchhiker's Guide to the Galaxy*. He never completed on time; in fact he usually had not started work at all by delivery time. His final editor booked him into a suite of an expensive hotel, moved in with him and did not move out until Douglas had finished the book. Ironically, even though he had started 'late', he finished a few weeks after delivery date and therefore, in that respect, outperformed most authors.

For the average editor, life is much more mundane. Dealing with slippage means setting up a system of checks and progress chasing which can cut down on the number of horrible surprises that sometimes arise if you keep your authors too much at arm's length during the writing process.

One thing must be made absolutely clear, however. You can never eliminate slippage. Books are written by authors who, as human beings, are susceptible to life events and moods. They can be delayed by illness or accidents, or by bereavement, or by a change of job, or by a divorce – experienced editors have come across every conceivable situation leading to a typescript being delayed. Because life does not always go to plan, neither do delivery dates. The best an editor can hope for is to limit the damage done when an author does not deliver as contracted.

There are some publishing houses that have produced booklets for authors that deal precisely with the issue of delivering books on time and why it is important. Whilst that is an extremely sensible move, one cannot guarantee that an author will read the booklet, and authors who do read it might regard themselves as somehow being exempt. We are here talking about special pleading. It is therefore advisable for an editor to take up a proactive position when dealing with slippage.

More on slippage, and how to avoid it, is dealt with later in this chapter.

SYSTEMS FOR PROGRESS CHASING

Start as you mean to go on. When the terms and conditions of the contract are being agreed, work out a system for liaison that is comfortable for both parties. Make it clear to the author that you will be contacting him or her from time to time and that you are vitally interested in keeping a progress check on the writing. Remember, however, that you are not just working with schedules here, you are also discussing ways in which you can support the author with his or her writing.

Some authors will actually ask for your involvement in the writing process. They will tell you that it is going to be vital that you read each chapter as it is finished and that they will need your comments. If that is what they want and need to produce a good book, then that is what you are going to offer. It may seem like yet another burden on you, but it will give you very good assurance that the author is at work on the book as the chapters gradually roll in. Others will ask what you want: do you want to read each chapter or do you want to wait until the end? You can feel reasonably encouraged by these authors because they are showing some understanding of working with their editor and have some ideas of their editor's needs too.

Most authors do not comment on liaison. As far as they are concerned, they are simply going off to write the book and you will hear from them when they are ready. It is a good principle to raise the question of liaison, however, because in discussing ways and means of keeping in touch and giving encouragement, you will uncover the author's attitude to the process of writing and that attitude should very much determine the plans you make to monitor him or her. The ease and efficiency of email has made the business of keeping in touch so easy.

TIMEFRAMES FOR PROGRESS CHASING

The length of time contracted for the book to be written will determine the progress chasing to be done.

1 If the author is going to write within twelve months, it is advisable to give him or her a ring or send an email every couple of months. It goes almost without saying that the general tone at this stage should be nothing less than friendly enthusiasm. Save the heavy stuff until you need it. In the last month before delivery date, shorten the period between contact times. You might find yourself ringing or emailing the author once a week. Play it by ear. If the author seems irritated by this, you have to decide on whether you are simply getting in the way or whether the author is feeling guilty because he or she is behind schedule. You must use as much common sense as psychology about this because each author and situation is different. The objective is that the author should be made aware of your need to have the typescript on time.

2 In the gestation period for a specialist book, it is necessary to start slowly and gradually build up the pressure. Suppose that your author has two years in which to produce the typescript. For the first eighteen months, a friendly email or phone call enquiring how things are going could be sent out every three months. For the last six months, switch to monthly calls or emails, increasing their frequency in the

month before delivery date. Again, use common sense as you gauge the author's reaction to these enquiries.

3 Remember to enquire about items that could hold up delivery, such as clearing permissions or waiting for material from secondary sources. The author should understand that none of this should be left to the last minute.

Whatever risks are involved in 'bothering' the author, they are worthwhile because you will uncover information not just about the progress of the typescript but also about the author which is infinitely better than both of you sitting in silence, guessing what the other one is up to. It is also important to repeat that nothing but friendly concern and enthusiasm should colour your approach. You may be policing your author, but ideally he or she should not notice it.

Technology makes liaison and progress chasing easy. Databases of forward titles can be flagged so that one key stroke can display which titles should be chased and when. In this way the editor can keep on top of his or her forward programme.

For editors working on projects (in educational, textbook and reference publishing as mentioned in Chapter 2), contact with authors through telephone calls and letters will not be good enough. Regular team meetings are essential. Material already written needs to be read by various members of the team, illustrations have to be scrutinised and agreed on, marketing plans will be in continual development and refinement. In addition, material will probably be trial-tested in the market to discern how successful the text is. In a sense, keeping in touch with the author is not an issue or a problem in this kind of publishing because the author is part of an ongoing team.

'SAFE' SCHEDULING

The word safe is in quote marks because nothing is 100 per cent safe in book publishing. As the cliché goes, if anything can go wrong, it will. By 'safe' is meant a schedule that has some extra time built into it should something go wrong.

1 If the contract specifies June delivery, present an in-house schedule that has a period of time added. In any case, extra time must be added in for receiving, reading and checking the manuscript. If the book is a specialist one, that might take some weeks because an opinion on the manuscript from an outside adviser is required and most advisers will require several weeks to read a manuscript carefully. However, in addition to the time needed for these 'domestic' tasks, it is wise to

add on extra time to allow for the manuscript arriving late. By the time you are asked to write your budget for the following year, you will have had a fair amount of contact with the author and should have a reasonable grasp of how accurate delivery is going to be (unless you are unlucky and have been dealing with an author who has been dissembling all along, which is not unknown). The extra time is likely to be between one and three months. If the extra time is six months or over, then you are facing a drastically revised delivery date, or a blocked author, and another set of questions that flow from that.

2 Have two sets of forward programme. One contains a set of titles and their contracted delivery dates – your working schedule – the other the same set of titles but with another set of dates, i.e. the contracted dates plus some added time. This second list is what you show your colleagues who need a schedule of forward titles for planning production, marketing and so on. This is the 'safe' list because you have built in damage limitation.

3 If you are in the fortunate position of having more books available for delivery than needed to achieve your financial targets, hold back some of them from your forward schedule, listing only those that you know are effectively 'in the bag'. You will then meet your targets and will also impress colleagues with a seeming ability to control authors.

PROVIDING APPROPRIATE AUTHOR SUPPORT

We all carry pictures of writers in our mind's eye. For authors who are writing fiction or poetry, we have a particular picture featuring temperament and mood and perhaps some sort of emotional agony – everything that is required to produce great writing! Then you discover that many of the most successful authors actually have a rather robust and down-to-earth attitude to writing: it's their job and they get on with it, in a rather matter-of-fact way. Usually it is the most gifted writers who have made the least fuss about writing their books and the second-rank authors who have made life difficult for themselves and everyone else involved in publication of their books.

All authors, however, need to be encouraged and nurtured – even the ones who don't seem to need support. There are few authors utterly indifferent to the interest and enthusiasm of an editor during the writing process. It is often surprising to see how strong the need is for feedback on the part of some of the most successful authors. Perhaps that is one of the reasons why they are successful: they are particularly aware that good communication is an elusive business.

A common mistake made by inexperienced editors working in specialist publishing is to assume that the writing of, for example, a scholarly book – academic, scientific or technical – is devoid of all the emotional processes that a 'real' writer, one of fiction or poetry, goes through. It isn't. The content of the writing may be very different but the process is very similar. Writing is a solitary business, whatever the genre. Nor are the strains of imaginary, creative work confined to fiction. A fiction writer may have a plot and characters to wrestle with. As great a task of the imagination faces the writer of scholarly non-fiction who has to marshall highly complicated sets of deductive reasoning, at the very least, along with supporting 'evidence'. Holding such intricate and difficult ideas and theories sufficiently well in one's mind in order to be able to manipulate them and communicate them is difficult. It is stressful work. It can produce emotional reactions in a non-fiction author just as powerful as in those whom we regard as 'real' writers.

Just because inexperienced editors see the material as 'dry', they overlook the nurturing, the encouragement which they should be supplying. It is as though they see the author writing the book in a state of complete emotional coldness because he or she is involved in an intellectual exercise. Perhaps some do but it is worth always assuming that most don't and remembering to treat them with considerable sensitivity – if you want to keep them as authors.

NURTURING VERSUS INDULGENCE

There is, however, a very thin dividing line between nurturing and indulgence. There is often little to choose between authors who simply get on with it, and hardly seem to need either your support or consultation, and others at the extreme opposite who are very demanding, indeed inappropriately so.

Nurturing is a process of taking care of the author in a way that supports him or her in their writing. The more genuine it is on the part of the editor, the more effective it is. Keeping in touch with your author is not simply monitoring the progress he or she is making; it is also a way of giving encouragement and guidance. It can mean reading and commenting constructively on the material the author is producing; giving empathetic understanding of the solitary and often difficult task in which the author is engaged; conveying market information which you have come across which the author might find useful or encouraging; giving news about your publishing house's activities that might be relevant to his or her book.

Equally importantly, be prepared to chivvy the authors when they seem to have lost their way – whether it is over the content or the speed with which they are writing.

AUTHOR ANXIETY

Writing books is a difficult process and the author can sometimes suffer as a consequence. Therein lie dangers for the editor because there are authors who simply cannot handle their own anxiety about what they are doing. These are the ones who will want to be indulged. When you have just signed a contract with an author you have not published before, you do not truly know what lies ahead. If you have done your work of evaluating and signing up a book professionally, courteously, but maintaining some sense of distance between yourself and the author, the more personal and psychological aspects of the relationship have yet to emerge. There is a certain amount of celebration in the air too: the book has been accepted, a contract has been signed.

Every author is different. Authors with potential for being indulged have one thing in common – they want excessive amounts of contact with the editor. They want to hear from you constantly and they want to tell you what a hard time they are having. Especially, they will tell you about the things that are getting in the way of their writing. Find ways of gently reverting to that more formal style in which you did business before the contract was signed. It does not involve being rude to the author, just a little more reserved and distant than you might naturally be. It is worth gritting your teeth about this because if you don't, the chances are that by delivery date you will have an author who certainly has not finished the manuscript on time, has got used to ringing you on every occasion he or she hits even the mildest form of writing block, and thinks this kind of behaviour between editor and author is *normal*. You will regret you ever indulged the author; you will regret you ever met that author.

In the next chapter, which covers delivery date to publication, another set of behaviours is encountered with authors which can also be classified under the general heading of author anxiety, and which also beg for the kind of indulgence that is to be avoided.

PLANNING AHEAD FOR DELIVERY DATE

Part of this chapter has already been spent on planning ahead in a general fashion but it is worth covering some of the specifics that go into this.

GUIDELINES FOR REVISING BUDGETS

Budgets are the key to keeping typescripts on target both for timing and for the financial parameters that surround a book. They are almost always prepared ahead of the appearance of the publishing programme and consist of all the books you intend to publish in the year ahead. You must assess the situation for each individual book.

Time has inevitably passed since the book was signed up. You must now ask, when revising the budget, whether anything has changed.

Print run

Should the print run remain as originally proposed or has the market shifted in any way up or down? Consult recent sales figures for similar books before finally committing yourself to a print run. In many houses the print run is set in discussion with other colleagues, especially in marketing, but check figures for yourself beforehand.

Pricing

When working in a time of inflation, the chances are the price should rise considerably from the one proposed when the book was contracted. Even if inflation isn't critical, if two or three years have elapsed since the contract was signed, do not simply transfer the proposed price to the revised budget. Adjust up because the cost of producing books will almost certainly have risen. It may also be necessary to recost some books at this stage.

Home and export sales

When you proposed the book for publication and presented a profit and loss account for it, assumptions will have been made about home and export sales. Do these assumptions still hold up today or has the balance between sales made at home and abroad changed? It does matter. The discounts given away on home and export sales differ considerably and if that balance is not projected accurately, your revenue will be very different from what was budgeted.

Discounts

Discounts can also change considerably between contract time and delivery date. Several things could have happened. For example, if you are a professional publisher you might find that your company's progressive move into direct mail has meant that your average discounts are actually diminishing. Or (unfortunately even more likely), if you are a consumer books publisher, pressure in the book shops has meant that booksellers are demanding even higher discounts. Since the abolition of the Net Book Agreement, the whole area of discounting is now volatile. For specialist publishers, if there has been a distinct change in the trading relationship with the main overseas distributors, you need to take that into account if discounts are affected.

Sub-rights

Since the book was commissioned the sub-rights manager has done a brilliant serialisation deal, or a co-publication deal, that is going to bring in unplanned and much appreciated income in the first year of the book's life. That must be written into its budget.

Checking print runs, pricing and discounts to ensure that they still hold good seems so basic that it should not need to be mentioned. Unfortunately, budgets are often thrown together at great speed and under pressure, and many editors, especially inexperienced ones, have been known simply to go to their files and solemnly and accurately copy down all the information that held good for that book when it was contracted, perhaps as much as three years ago. You may work in a publishing house where there are rolling revenue plans that get regularly updated. In this case it should be possible to avoid letting your information get out of date.

IN-HOUSE SCHEDULES

Perhaps the majority of your books will go through the publication process in a straightforward fashion. In every type of publishing there are exceptions and the most common one is creating a schedule for a book where 'time is of the essence'. Whether the book has to come out in good time for Christmas, or the Bologna Book Fair, or Frankfurt, or the beginning of the school year, or if it is a particularly high revenue earner, it is absolutely essential that nothing in house impedes its progress through to that special publication date. It is necessary to plan ahead to remind your colleagues in sub-editorial, production and design of its imminent arrival. These departments in particular are crucial because they are going to make the book. The sales force will also need alerting of this special book as early as possible in order to hit the market at the opportune moment.

Even if a book is not receiving this kind of focused treatment, the rolling schedules drawn up for production and design should be checked on a regular basis and through informal discussion with your colleagues in those departments, you can enquire about the progress of your books. An editor who is alert to what is happening to the books is more likely to receive co-operation than one who is neglectful.

FAST-TRACK BOOKS

There is another class of book that goes through the house on a deliberately fast track. We hear about books that are written, produced and published within a couple of weeks – and we are filled with wonder. No house can sustain more than one of these on an occasional basis because the effort involved is too great. All types of publishing houses are offered books where the writing and publication processes by necessity have to be much shorter than normal. Talk to a consumer books editor and he or she will probably say that a four- to five-month publication schedule is normal. Talk to an academic editor and you will find that he or she may be accustomed to working to nine- to twelve-month schedules. Whatever the in-house norm, and however you judge what is your own particular fast track, it is absolutely necessary to keep all departments fully in the picture and that all parts of the process are planned beforehand.

- Advise sub-editorial of the exact arrival of the manuscript so that the copy-editor is ready to start as soon as it has arrived and has been approved. The copy-editor will need to know the precise date for completing work on the text.
- If there are queries for the author to answer as a result of the copy-editing, he or she must be told the dates by which those queries have to be turned around.
- The design department has to have the right designer for the job, ready and briefed ahead.
- Production needs to know the precise day on which the manuscript will arrive in their department and to make arrangements for it to be marked up for the printer. Most importantly, the printer needs to be given an absolutely reliable date for receiving the disk for setting and printing. If disks do not arrive on time, printers will not hang around waiting. They will get on with the next project to hand and your printing slot is lost.
- You need to know when proofs are coming and the author has to be advised of the date and how long he or she has to read them.
- If the book needs an index, the indexer must be fixed up in advance, with a schedule.

It is a logistical campaign and needs to be seen that way. It is a campaign that is likely to be handled in large measure by your colleagues in sub-editorial, but it is your job to facilitate matters between the author and your colleagues and to play your full agreed part in it.

If you leave it to delivery day to remind your colleagues that they have a fast-track book on their hands do not be surprised if they make their frustration and anger known, and then prepare to be extremely grateful if they rescue you from your own bad organisation. Too often production are expected to work miracles for editors who are too thoughtless or lazy to plan ahead, or on account of late delivery. Do always keep them informed.

SPECIAL ARRANGEMENTS

There can be many. When preparing for delivery ask what – in addition to everything else – constitutes something special about this book, in terms of its needs? What else needs thinking about? Here are some examples:

- Early jackets for a marketing and promotion campaign. Find out when jacket proofs are going to be required and work backwards from there. Begin with the work of writing cover blurbs as a priority especially if endorsements are to be sought to go on the cover or jacket.
- Co-publication requires that you have the typescript, figures and schedule ready to go to the co-publisher the moment they are available. Set up early systems for liaison with the co-publisher's production department if you are going to be producing the book for them, giving them estimated dates for proofs, bound copies and shipping.
- Is the typescript going to be very expensive to set, which will require that it be originated and printed overseas in order to hold costs? Remember to make plenty of allowance for this in the scheduling and talk it all through very carefully with the production department beforehand.
- Is there something different or special about the book that will cause it to fall out of the norm in other respects? For example, does it need its own customised design? Does it need to be printed on special paper? Is clearance needed on an illustration for the jacket that might be difficult to get, or where the owner could prove hard to track down? Many houses have standard book designs that are intended to speed the process of production. Anything that requires treatment outside of that standard should be flagged up by the editor.
- Any book that is going to require marketing and promotion that is outside the norm needs to be registered in the consciousness of your marketing colleagues well before delivery day. In a well-organised publishing house, it is highly likely that the senior marketing managers will be as attached as you are to a schedule of forward titles. They might get to you before you can get to them. Do not take this for granted, however. Take the time to alert them ahead to your special titles. Encourage them and do not take chances. Has the PR manager

really spotted the potential that this title has? Shouldn't you be telling the sales manager about your author's terrific local following so that the sales rep for that territory can mount a special campaign in the shops in that area? New textbooks for schools have to be targeted well in advance, co-ordinating mail shots with displays in local shops:
- Is this a book for a bookclub? Then the preliminary work needs to be done via the sub-rights department. Will the book sell very success-fully in Italy if an Italian translation can be arranged?
- Are there special events ahead which the publication of the book can mark, such as a new TV series, or a new film, or a special conference?
- Is your publishing house involved in direct mail? If so, lists of poten-tial buyers have to be researched and brokered well ahead and costed into the campaign. Telemarketing, for example, requires detailed plan-ning ahead since by its nature it is expensive and time-consuming.

There are so many things that can come under the category of special arrangements. The main point to get across is that you must work ahead, listing all these needs, then begin the process of making them happen. The chances are that these special things might take place anyway, but they will be that bit more effective if they are planned and initiated by you rather than stumbled across by someone else.

However well organised you are, you can still fall victim to some of the commonest problems that beset editors in this phase of the publishing process.

SLIPPAGE

Slippage is by far and away the most damaging issue connected with editorial work. The following are the main effects of slippage:

- The manuscript is inevitably going to be too long – a late manuscript is commonly an over-length manuscript.
- The book will be published far later than planned and may no longer be timely.
- Costs will have risen.
- It might be necessary to change format because of the foregoing.
- Your reputation as a professional editor will slip with the book.
- Your budget will be inaccurate because your revenues and costs for the book have been calculated in respect of the parameters set out when it was accepted for publication and was contracted.
- Your colleagues in sub-editorial, marketing and production will have had their carefully laid plans upset because the book did not arrive as planned.

- The market for the book may have changed in the meantime, rendering the book a failure. Educational publishers are particularly sensitive about getting their books out on time because a major curriculum change can be disastrous for a title that appears too late.
- The book may miss the all-important Christmas market or the beginning of the academic year, or a competitive title may be launched ahead of yours.
- Consider the multiplier effect in any publishing house when slippage takes place across the board: a large house with perhaps 30 or more editors each with, in all probability, three books running late (at least!) has 90 books at risk in any given year, throwing revenue plans into disarray.

The key to this potential embarrassment is, as stated before, to 'plan' for slippage. It cannot be eliminated but the damage that is caused can be limited if you recognise and acknowledge that books do slip.

GUIDELINES ON AVOIDING SLIPPAGE

If these guidelines are followed there is a better chance of avoiding chaos.

- Emphasise to authors, at contract stage, that you expect and require them to deliver on time. Get the author to put the delivery date in his or her diary and put it in yours too.
- Construct a schedule for progress chasing at regular intervals.
- Never ignore signs that the author may be running late. Seek early confirmation of the real situation and adjust your schedules accordingly.
- Always build extra time into your schedules even if the book is expected on the contracted delivery date. There can sometimes be last-minute, unforeseen hitches at the author's end.
- Emphasise to authors that it is vital they send off permissions letters to copyright holders the moment they have decided to use secondary material. Waiting for clearance, which has been sought too late, can hold up a book significantly.
- Allow sufficient time for you (and your adviser if you need one) to read the typescript.
- Build in time for the author to make revisions, especially if the author is an untried one.
- Construct two schedules: an official version that has time built into it, and will be circulated to colleagues, and your own version, based on contracted, or revised, dates.
- Discipline yourself to put on your schedules only books whose safe arrival you can account for. Do not include those whose status is speculative.

- Be prepared to remind the author of the obligation of the contract. In very difficult situations consider imposing financial penalties, but only after discussion with your senior colleagues.

EDUCATING AUTHORS ABOUT THE CONSEQUENCES OF SLIPPAGE

Every now and then, an author will be encountered who seems to flaunt all rules of decency. Whatever you do, whatever agreements you think you have made, you cannot get this typescript in.

Anyone who has been in publishing for some time will have wonderful examples of authors' 'excuses'. There was the author whose infected contact lenses turned him blind for the precise two weeks allowed for a tight proof schedule. Another who fell asleep in bed with the electric blanket on and claimed to have singed the typescript he was working on. Yet another who delivered his manuscript 23 years late and complained about being harassed.

There are two effective approaches to educating authors about the importance of delivering their books on time:

1 Get the author to understand the context in which the book is slipping. Remember, up until now, the only person that the author has met in the publishing house is you. The chances are that it will always be like that. You are the person to whom the author relates. Marketing, production and sales are rather shadowy figures to most authors. Succinctly, you represent the publishing house. Therefore, if you somehow relay a message that you can live with the slippage, the author will assume that the publishing house can too.

2 Rarely do authors understand how each department interconnects and how, if something goes wrong in one department, it can have a knock-on effect in the others. It is worth pointing out to the late deliverer that the existence of his or her book is already known to production, marketing, sales and so on; that the title stands on everyone's forward publishing programmes. Indeed, there is a whole mass of people – not just you the editor – who are wondering just exactly when the book is going to turn up. If you really want to make the author think twice about this, point out how a book (and an author) can acquire a reputation even before its publication date – in this case for, seemingly, being destined never to appear. Furthermore, since the whole publishing process requires a huge effort on everyone's part to haul and push the book successfully into the market-place, the last thing that any book jostling for position in the publishing programme needs is any kind of negative association in the minds of those who are going to be making the effort.

Communicating the above should take place right at the beginning of the process, when signing the contract and laying the ground rules with the author. It is worth taking the time right at the beginning to put the author in the picture in the fullest sense. It might save an awful lot of trouble later.

CONFLICT BETWEEN AUTHORS

Although editors worry a lot about rows between themselves and authors, bitter conflict sometimes arises between two authors or between members of a team of authors. Authors elect to write a book jointly and sometimes (especially on those large projects) they are put together by the publisher. They fall out because one is slower than the other in producing the work; because one thinks the other one's work is not up to scratch; because they develop a simple dislike of each other while working under the strain of producing a book together. This can happen not just between authors but also between photographers or illustrators and the text writer.

Inevitable delays can be expected because of this, and in the case of major conflict, the whole book or project can disintegrate. Occasionally this conflict manifests itself at delivery date when there is disagreement about whose name is to appear first on the cover. Unless one of them is prepared eventually to concede (probably after a great deal of aggravation) that the lion's share was done by the other, then you can only retreat to the good old-fashioned rule of thumb: alphabetical order. Your preference, of course, is that the more senior, better-known author's name should appear first – for obvious commercial reasons – but once you enter into arguments about 'fairness', which are bound to ensue, it is sometimes difficult to hold that line. You can try stipulating as a condition of contract that the senior author appears first but, of course, if they are on a par, you are stuck with the same problem. However, do not spend too much time on this issue – a book cannot be held up indefinitely because of this. Make your mind up and get on with it, knowing that whatever is decided you cannot avoid mortally offending one of them.

If two authors engaged on a large project have fallen out, you will probably find out about it quite early on because the nature of publishing requires that you meet the authors on a regular basis. If the situation seems irretrievable, buy off the recalcitrant one and find a substitute author very quickly, but only when you have thoroughly analysed what the surviving author needs in terms of a workmate.

CONFLICT BETWEEN AUTHOR AND EDITOR

Alas, conflict can also break out between you and your author. If you are doing your job professionally, then you must not let a clash of personality get in the way. However much you may dislike your author, you have to put that behind you and concentrate on the book. A clash over content or style is a different matter.

If an impasse develops, seek out corroboration of your views via your colleagues and/or your advisers. It will be far easier to persuade authors to change their approach if you have good evidence from third parties to show them. If all fails, you may be faced with the consequence of losing the book, and therefore the author. In the case of a first-time writer, this failure – although difficult to bear – may be tolerable. For an important author with an established record, a potential failure of this sort may be too risky – there is a very strong chance that the author will find another, willing publisher for the book. If you find yourself in this position, seek the advice of your senior colleagues before proceeding any further.

FAILURE TO DELIVER

Every editor has them and they basically take one of two forms.

WRITER'S BLOCK

One might as well accept as part and parcel of the process that there is a tiny minority of authors who desperately want to write a book but, when it comes to it, just find it all too difficult. It may be nothing to do with ability or creativity but is more likely to be connected with inhibition and anxiety. Writing a book is hard work and, when it is published, it is a very public thing to have done. Everyone can read the author's thoughts, judge his ideas, assess her creativity and form an opinion of their intellect. The author is exposed. For some, the reality is simply too much. They get struck by writer's block; they revise and revise hoping to reach perfection; they simply feel too scared to hand the thing over.

Some authors fail to complete for quite mundane reasons but they are rather straightforward about this. They simply give the reasons and ask to return the contract. But when some books slip and slip and the author cannot quite be honest with you, it is because he or she finds it too difficult to accept the truth: that completing the book has just gone beyond him or her. There are three ways one can approach this:

- Avoid too many 'sympathetic' conversations with an author, listening with concern to the problems that are getting in the way. They usually sound plausible. The editor must not collude in this.

- When delivery date fails to materialise for the third or fourth time, be brave and face up to the truth. The author is not going to complete. Terminate the contract. You might be surprised to find a manuscript on your desk not long after. Sometimes the author's ego is so outraged by your actions as to be forced to complete.
- Remember to explain firmly to the author the consequences of prolonging slippage. There are consequences for you, for the house, and for the author. If the book is going to be any later arriving, unfortunately it will become stigmatised – the book that no one thought would ever turn up.

Whatever the outcome at the very least you have now settled the situation that has been highly ambiguous and has probably caused you a lot of uncertainty and even anxiety. That will free you to do other more constructive work. 'Failure to show up' happens in every single sector of publishing. A common challenge for all editors is to be honest and brave enough to recognise a hopeless situation, and then let go of it.

THE BOOK THAT IS NOT WHAT YOU CONTRACTED

The second most common problem is the book that on delivery turns out to be neither what you expected nor what you wanted. At proposal time, you and the author were in complete agreement about the book on offer. Somewhere along the way the author has either deviated from the original proposal or has not written the material the way you envisaged it. If you are fortunate, the author will be sensitive to your reactions and will be prepared to rewrite, to your satisfaction.

- A work of fiction cannot be rewritten in this way, although many works of fiction can and do benefit from a strong editorial treatment. The book will have to be accepted on its own merits, unless you feel very strongly that it is now a poor one, in which case you need to enlist the support of your colleagues and the author's agent. If both sets of parties remain in disagreement, the agent is likely to accept releasing the author from the contract, provided that he or she is able to find another publisher prepared to take the book on. If they fail to do that, because other publishers also find the book unattractive, then you have made and won your point and are in a strong position to insist on breaking the contract.
- For non-fiction books, the position should be easier to handle because considered points can be made about content that are much more difficult to make about the sometimes indefinable qualities of good or bad fiction-writing. Arm yourself with detailed comments on the

manuscript, preferably backed up by comments from colleagues and advisers, and be prepared to work through all of them with the author (and agent). If you have done your work properly, with all reason, you are likely to receive co-operation from the author and agent. If a true impasse develops, follow the procedures just outlined for fiction. Offer the author the chance to find another publisher.

DEALING WITH UNSATISFACTORY WRITING

QUALITY

This can be tricky, if you think it is bad but the author thinks it is good!

- *Specialist publishers* can resort to 'expert opinion'. Specialist publishers rarely publish or commission books without the independent opinions of acknowledged experts. However, many aggrieved authors, on receiving an anonymous critical opinion on a typescript, will find many ways, some of them quite ingenious, for questioning the quality of the reader's report itself. Be prepared to take several reports if you find yourself dealing with an author who is questioning your judgement and that of your adviser.
- *Consumer books editors* do not have the same kind of independent 'expertise' to hand, although most publishers pay 'readers' to look at scripts for them. If you need back-up for your opinion, you can look to these readers for their judgement but in most cases, it will be the opinions of colleagues in marketing and sales on which you are likely to rely. Remember, however, that in consumer books publishing the author is likely to be writing for a living and is equally likely to have a literary agent acting on his or her behalf. Literary agents are very good at fighting for the rights of their authors and will need a lot of convincing, especially if the agent has read the manuscript immediately prior to delivery and considers it good enough to go off to the publisher.
- Always give an author an adequate set of reasons for stating your unwillingness to publish a contracted typescript. Even if the typescript is truly bad, the author is still likely to have put a lot of work into writing it and will probably be shocked as well as disappointed at being rejected. You should expect adverse reaction and if you do not make your reasons for rejection entirely clear, frankly, you are asking for trouble.

Never allow yourself to be bullied or compromised into publishing a book which you know is not up to scratch. Not only will the writer's reputation be sullied by its appearance in print, so will that of your publishing house, and your own.

DEVIATION FROM THE PUBLISHING PROPOSAL

If you have been doing your work properly in the run-up to delivery date, being in touch reasonably frequently with the author, this kind of surprise is unlikely to be sprung on you. However, there are some authors who become very secretive indeed during the course of writing a book. They might be quite diligent about telling you how many words they have written, whether they are on schedule or not, but are unwilling or unable to talk to you about content. This could be because they find the whole experience so personal to themselves that they do not want to talk about what they are writing. Sometimes, however, the book seems to run away from them and turns into something else along the way.

- If the delivered typescript has deviated from the original proposal, then make it clear to the author straight away that you are now being asked to consider a new book. This is not the book contracted and you therefore have to go through the entire process of appraisal again. The author must be patient because, contractually, he or she does not have a leg to stand on. With luck, you might discover that a good, or even better, book is to hand. If not, then you have double the reason to return the typescript.
- If you *commissioned* an author to write a specific book, and nothing else, there is no question about it: you are entirely within your rights to reject anything that is substantially different from what you contracted.

LENGTH

Over-long typescripts have already been considered in the previous chapter (page 44) but it is worth recalling that they also represent deviations from the contracted deal.

Occasionally you will take delivery of a typescript that is massively over-length but is so outstandingly good that you know you cannot take a hatchet to it. If you have the courage of your conviction, you will publish it at that length, and at the consequent higher price, but if your faith in it is rewarded, you will enjoy its sales and its higher revenues. But be careful not to deceive yourself. Very big books, which swallow up large amounts of production investment, have got to be very good.

If a substantially under-length typescript arrives, it usually means one thing: the author has not covered the subject adequately and you will have to address that carefully with him or her. On the other hand, you might discover that the author has a (rare) talent for concise but effective writing. In which case, press on. If it is a really good book you can still price it at the level you envisaged but bulk it out to look like good value for money.

GUIDELINES FOR REJECTING UNSATISFACTORY MANUSCRIPTS

- If the book deviates from the contracted proposal on length, content or style, resolve to tackle this with the author immediately. Do not live in hope by letting it proceed as it is. You are just delaying the moment when the problem will fully emerge and has to be resolved.
- If length is the problem, tell the author what needs to be added or cut. If the author does not understand the financial consequences, especially those caused by over-length books, explain them in detail. If the author is unwilling to cut, offer the choice of either cutting the length or accepting a lower royalty.
- If the problem is content, always give the author sight of advisers' reports. If this is not appropriate to your sector of publishing, give the author detailed comments – your own and those of other colleagues.
- Be prepared to spend time with the author, and the agent if one is involved, talking through the problems as you see them. Do not conduct such negotiations at arm's length. It is bound to lead to misunderstandings.
- If an impasse develops, do not be afraid to remind the author that you have a legally binding contract that gives you the right to reject a book if it is unsatisfactory. However, that cuts both ways. You have to provide good evidence for its being unsatisfactory.
- Many authors, when reminded that you are legally entitled to reject a book, will do their best to comply with your wishes. Some cannot because they are unable to revise the manuscript to the required standard. If they fail after two or three attempts, sever the contract. However much they object, the majority of authors will accept the outcome.
- If the author simply refuses to comply, state your intention to sever the contract. Put it in writing, listing all the problems with the delivered book and appending colleagues' or advisers' reports. Give the author two weeks to reply. There is risk involved because if the author still refuses to give way, you must now go ahead and terminate the contract. If this does happen, but you have been scrupulous in naming

carefully the problems the book has posed, you are at the very least on firm ground. Alas, you have also lost your book – a book you did not want the way it turned out, but better that than to proceed with a book that will fail. Sometimes, however, this explicit threat will cause the author to re-think and comply.

- If the author makes legal threats, however unnerving, remember that few do more than threaten. And if he or she does translate threats into legal action, you will have your evidence to hand.
- Put everything in writing, however easy it might seem to 'sort things out' over the telephone.
- Always consult your senior colleagues every step of the way if you ever find yourself in this position. Directors of publishing houses do not like being made to defend something they know little about.

RECOUPING ADVANCES

There are financial considerations to be borne in mind in this situation. If an advance has been paid, a decision will be needed about whether it should be returned or not – unless the contract states it is non-returnable.

- Some specialist publishers, who hand out small advances, will allow the author to keep them on the understanding that the amount is small and that the author may have put a lot of work into something that has, sadly, failed.
- For consumer books publishers, quite substantial amounts may have been paid out and a less kindly eye is bound to be turned on losses of this sort. If agents are involved, this will have to be negotiated with them.
- Whatever the publishing sector, make sure you understand the company's policy in relation to advances and always refer the situation upwards to senior colleagues, both for advice and guidance, and to keep them in the picture. Remember that the contract with the author is a legal document and that it may be necessary to take legal remedies. If that happens, you will most certainly need the support and direction of your manager.
- When the author refuses, when requested, to return the advance, it does unhappily remind you only too forcibly of your own responsibility for the company's money. It happens to even the most professional and diligent editors but it should reinforce for everyone, when authorising advances, that they constitute money that the company may not see again.

CASE STUDY

A major international publisher with a strong presence in the education market decided to make a massive investment of £100,000 (plant costs) for an upper level school book that would also be suitable for foundation degree courses at British universities. The subject area was chemistry. The publishers reasoned that a good-quality book would be capable of making the cross-over. In view of that cross-over, they decided to pair a respected school book author with a university professor with no real writing track record outside authorship of academic papers. They were trying hard to find a balance of science knowledge and literacy within the partnership.

When the two co-authors swapped their first chapters for review, it was clear that they were coming to the project from very different approaches. The school author was willing to let students see 'the exciting content even if they can't understand chemistry yet': 'Trust me, you will learn this later.' The academic felt very strongly that the readers had to understand all underlying theories and that these must be presented to them first.

After much to-ing and fro-ing and discussion, the academic left the project feeling that he was being compromised, and so was his subject, by the general approach. The publishers brought in a replacement author.

The book was delayed as a consequence, and in order to catch up for lost time and try to keep the project to a sensible time-scale, yet a third author was brought in. This also added to the costs.

Nevertheless, when the book was launched, it became a market leader in its field, and still is.

QUESTION

Would you have attempted a cross-over approach in the first place? Harry Potter apart, it is very difficult to write for two levels and it is generally thought that different levels have different needs. What steps would you have taken to avoid the confrontation that inevitably took place between the two authors? Was this a good example of harnessing a racehorse to a milk float? How might you have dealt with negotiations between the two authors? Would you have stuck with the school book writer instead of the university chemistry professor, and why?

Managing the publication process   5

In this chapter we are going to be covering:

- explaining the publication process to the author
- taking delivery of typescripts
- liaison with colleagues over sub-editorial and production details
- doing your paperwork
- blurb writing
- co-publications and distribution arrangements
- briefing designers
- providing marketing with full and relevant information
- sales conference presentations
- involving your authors appropriately
- publication day
- dealing with inappropriate behaviour

After the many imponderables covered in the last two chapters, we now turn to an area that will seem more grounded than what has gone before – the process of 'caretaking' typescripts through to publication date and just beyond. In an overstretched, competitive place such as a publishing office, the one unifying factor is the book and, by extension, its 'keeper', the editor. When an editor remains very firmly involved in the publication process, not only will the book be better published, the editor will remain at the centre of a successful team which can go on to repeat those successes with future books.

The editor's job is certainly not finished because the typescript has arrived, although it is tempting to dump it on others because there are new titles to be commissioned and more finished typescripts to receive. Your responsibility is continual even if your colleagues now take over stages of the book's progress through sub-editorial, production and marketing, all of which require special skills. The editor is still the repository of more information about the book than anyone else in the publishing house and that information must be shared with everyone else who is working on it.

EXPLAINING THE PUBLICATION PROCESS TO THE AUTHOR

The chances are that your publishing house produces a small booklet that explains to authors the processes that books go through when they are in production. Wise and helpful though that is, you can probably have more of an effect on your author if you can spare the time to take him or her through the procedures face-to-face. You might combine this with a meeting on delivery day, or through another opportunity that could present itself.

Remember that only experienced authors have some understanding of the production process, and even some of them have formed only a partial view for one reason or another. For the rest it seems that their typescripts are entering a black hole. What is going to happen? When? Who will be involved? What about the jacket? These are the typical kinds of question that are going through the author's mind.

Take time to explain to the author:

- When copy-editing takes place and what it entails.
- How long he or she is likely to wait before receiving queries on the typescript.
- The importance of returning answers by the date given.
- When proofs will arrive, and what the author's responsibilities will be.
- The importance of returning corrected proofs by the deadline given.
- That the index has to be prepared (if appropriate). At this point, it may prove necessary to reassure the author that professional indexers are more than capable of providing good indexes for books in subjects for which they do not have expert knowledge.
- If the author anticipates wanting to compile the index personally, warn him or her that indexes are prepared at the same time as proofs are read; ask if he or she will honestly be able to do both jobs.
- That if they do not hear from their publishers for some time, they should not assume that nothing is happening. Some do. Tell them that they will be contacted when their input is required, which will be almost entirely with the processes of copy-editing and proof-reading.
- How jacket design works, and quietly, and very politely, remind them that – contractually – the publisher has responsibility for designing

the jacket/cover (apart from exceptional cases involving very high-profile authors). You can also explain to them about how many colours you can afford to use and why, and about the expense involved in clearing permissions for using fine art or famous photographs. Show them attractive jackets where only two or three colours have been used. It is good policy to ask for the author's view on the kind of image he or she would like to see on the jacket/cover. The whole area of jackets, and how authors perceive them, is a super-charged area. If you attempt to keep the author out completely, you are building up trouble for yourself. Imagine if you wrote a book and someone said to you about the jacket, 'It's none of your damn business.' This, essentially, is what happens far too often. If you ask the author's opinion, he or she will feel involved, and quite often when asked for an opinion, does not have one. But by asking, you can avoid that sense of being kept out of things. Marketing's views will always be a strong ally for you in any difference of opinion between you and the author over the jacket.

- How marketing and promotion works, and the importance of the authors' questionnaire in helping to inform a campaign.

Having done this, you have done the groundwork for perhaps a more trouble-free experience of the publication process, both for you and the author.

EXAMINATION OF TYPESCRIPTS

An outsider would be very surprised to hear that there is a surprising number of editors who, when forced to, will admit that more often than not, they do not read delivered typescripts – or if they do, read only bits of them. The reason given is pressure of work, and in some houses with very big publishing programmes, this is a genuine reason. In an academic house with a monograph programme, it is possible that an editor might be responsible for 75 titles or more per year. To attempt to read all of them *and* carry out all the responsibilities connected with one's work as an editor, is impossible. In any case, monographs simply do not get the full treatment – in production and marketing terms – that most books do, and close familiarity with content is not so essential. If you are an editor operating at another level of specialist publishing, it is still possible to avoid reading typescripts as one relies on outside experts to evaluate the quality of scholarship, for example. That outside reading can, in the editor's mind, substitute for his or her own reading.

Unless you are working for a high through-put house, such as a monograph publisher, it is always advisable to read the manuscript yourself.

Familiarity with the text will help you with any difficulties that might befall the book as it passes through the house. It will certainly convey conviction when you talk about it – especially if you are going to present it at a sales conference. If you are able to talk about the book with conviction your colleagues will take it seriously. How could you expect them to take your book seriously if you transparently have not bothered to read it? It is certainly worth demonstrating to the author that you have read it, particularly authors whom you want to keep.

If you are not a monograph publisher, but your workload is very heavy, try at least to read the beginning and conclusion of the typescript.

Finally, if an advance is payable on delivery, do not pay it until you have satisfied yourself that the content is, at the very least, acceptable to you.

CHECKLIST FOR TYPESCRIPTS

1 Read as much of the typescript as you can for content, and, for a specialist publisher, enlist an outside expert to advise on its quality. Act on advice given, and on your own suggestions for improvement. Later in this chapter the problems that an unsatisfactory typescript presents will be discussed.

2 If you are an educational, textbook or reference publisher you will not only check the typescript yourself, but you will also share it with other members of the in-house team (especially marketing) to get their involvement and final approval. In consumer book publishing, marketing colleagues will certainly need to read the typescript if a big marketing campaign is planned.

3 Check that the typescript is complete. There are still authors who think it is fine to send in the whole typescript except for the introduction, or the conclusion, or the bibliography, or the illustrations, or sometimes ask to send it to you in chunks. Contracts specify that the typescript must be complete on delivery. A half-finished script is useless to a copy-editor who simply cannot start work if it is incomplete. Do not offload half-finished typescripts onto your colleagues in sub-editorial just to get them off your desk. The chances are their shelves are overflowing anyway and they do not need more piles of paper which, at this stage, are useless to them. A complete typescript comprises:
   (a) title page
   (b) contents page
   (c) preliminary matter if appropriate (e.g. acknowledgements, preface, dedication)

(d) all chapters

(e) notes (if appropriate)

(f) a complete list of references or bibliography

(g) other end matter, if appropriate, such as appendices or a glossary

(h) all illustrations, titled and marked precisely for their location in the text

(i) written evidence that permissions have been cleared.

Do not forget that checking also means checking that the manuscript is in house style; and if you are taking delivery on disk, that all the disks are present.

Clearing permissions

Unless you have come to a special agreement, it is the legal obligation of the author to clear permissions. Some authors will claim they are too busy to do it. Push them; often they simply do not want the bother of doing it or sometimes they are unsure about how it is done. You can instruct them on how to do this: for example, by the use of a stan-dardised letter to be sent to all copyright holders. If the author, after strenuous enquiries on your part, is clearly too busy to cope, be prepared to help out but also negotiate a fee to be paid for getting this work done. For example, it could be costed as an extra element to be added to the sub-editor's work and bill. You will need also to add in further time to your schedule as the process of clearing permissions can be lengthy.

Be especially vigilant that permission has been cleared for all the pur-poses to which you may wish eventually to put the material. You might find, for example, that permission has not been given to repurpose the material in another format. In which case, permission must be sought.

CHECKING OUT FACTS AND FIGURES

- If the book has facts (or purported facts) which could have legal conse-quences for the author and publisher if they are wrong, assure yourself of their accuracy.
- If the subject matter of the book is tendentious, again check the text for any content that is defamatory or libellous. A book about, let's say, corruption amongst the police, should automatically be sent to your literary lawyer for an opinion. Some books simply ask you to be alert but occasionally, lodged within something which seems quite harmless, lurks trouble: for example, a research monograph in anthro-pology that contained some extremely defamatory statements in one of its 150 footnotes.

Be alert to these potentially dangerous statements within a book and also train your sub-editors to watch out for them. You may also have a senior colleague who has had similar experiences in his or her career. Get their opinion on the matter. If there is any doubt, take the best legal advice available. Remember that most contracts contain a warranty clause in which the author guarantees to the publisher that nothing in the book is obscene, libellous, defamatory, an illegal use of someone else's copyright, and so on.

If a book does get onto the market, whose content causes offence, and a third party takes action against the author, you the publisher have to remove your stock from the shops and it cannot be sold until the case has been settled, which could take months. If the author loses the case, the stock is unsaleable and you have lost thousands of pounds for your company.

Remember in respect of libel that it is no defence to claim that material in your book is simply a reproduction of material which has already appeared in a newspaper or magazine. It is still a libel. A simple but crucial point of which many editors and authors are unaware.

- Lawyers are expensive people to consult. If you think you may be dealing with something libellous, contact your company's lawyer and outline the problem. Sometimes the whole thing can be cleared up over the phone. On other occasions the lawyer will ask to see the relevant pages. Ask about fees for this work. For advice on a few critical pages, you may be lucky enough to negotiate a modest fee. Discuss a sliding scale of fees for the amount of work involved. If you simply send the whole typescript, you are bound to end up paying something quite substantial. In some cases, where you are dealing with exceptionally inflammatory material, that will be necessary and probably worth every penny.

Essential reading for this whole area is *Publishing Law* by Hugh Jones and Chris Benson, a very clearly written and often enjoyable book on what one would expect to be a rather dry subject.

ADJUSTING TO CHANGING MARKET CONDITIONS

Do not assume that the market for the book has remained unchanged since you issued the contract. If the book has taken a year or more to be written, it is good practice to ask yourself if the anticipated sales of a year or two ago still hold good. Check this kind of sales information carefully and make adjustments to print runs and formats if the book no longer stands up to the profile you first drew up for it. In particular, if the author has delivered very late indeed and in all truth, the evidence from the market-place suggests that the sales for this type of book are sharply on the decline, do not proceed with publication.

The market has moved on, and most certainly, you will be contractually within your right to decline the manuscript on the grounds of late delivery. If the author, however, has delivered on time and to length and quality but the market has collapsed, you will have to recompense your author financially. The usual formula for this is that the author keeps the advance. If the author is a professional writer, and has an agent, you will probably have to make a substantial *ex gratia* payment that bears some relation to the royalties which the author might have earned in favourable circumstances.

LIAISON WITH SUB-EDITORIAL AND PRODUCTION

If the manuscript and the circumstances of the author are straightforward then there will be comparatively little information to give these departments, but the following examples are typical of the kind of information you need to pass on:

- Will the author be unable, for whatever reasons, to answer queries from the copy-editor or to read proofs on various dates?
- Does the author have any stylistic 'fancies' that you are prepared to accept in the text? For example, one group of distinguished authors laboured long and hard before deciding that the word 'psychoanalysis' should not have a hyphen in the middle of it. Some copy-editors would consider it essential. Another equally distinguished author insisted, for reasons that space precludes here, that the word 'sceptical' should be spelt 'skeptical' throughout the text. You need to note any agreed deviations from house style.

HOUSE STYLE

The author will have been given a style sheet which sets down the house style before embarking on the manuscript. For most of us, these are strict rules which should always be followed. There should always be good justification for deviation from them.

A house style has a twofold purpose. First, it has been in all probability developed over a period of years and has evolved into a kind of template for presenting material in a logical, accessible way. Second, at its heart lies consistency which certainly eases the process of sub-editorial and production work, and cuts down on the time and cost of both.

What about exceptions? For a British publisher taking delivery of a typescript from an American author, or vice versa, these days it is perfectly acceptable to leave the American or British spelling and punctuation as they are. Readers have become quite accustomed to reading either.

But if the author has wildly deviated from house style, return the typescript with a clear instruction to the author to put it into style and a firm date for returning it to you. You are acting absolutely within your rights to insist on this. If the author proves difficult, you can give him or her the option of having a sub-editor do the job but you must also make it clear that the author will have to pay for that work.

PRE-PRODUCTION ISSUES

- Is your author likely to be sensitive to any 'rewriting' that might occur during the sub-editorial process? Strictly speaking rewriting should not take place without consultation between the editor and the author but quite often this does happen because enthusiastic copy-editors think that they are improving the author's style. And sometimes they do. But consider this: the text is the author's, not yours and, quite seriously, how would you feel if someone started rewriting your letters or memos without asking you first? If, on closer inspection, the typescript does appear to have stylistic problems, then this is a matter that does need sorting out between editorial and sub-editorial, and an agreed approach to the author formulated. Remember, although there are some authors who might be offended at the suggestion that their writing needs some help, there are others who will fall on your neck with relief at the offer of a copy-editor who is prepared to use his or her skills on their behalf.
- Does the typescript need a special design or layout? If it does, then do not expect sub-editorial and production to figure it out as they go along. Sit down with them and take them through the basics of what is needed. For some very complicated books, it might be necessary to bring the author into the office for discussion with both departments.
- If the author is going to supply finished artwork, when is it coming, in what form is it coming, and will there be a cost incurred? If the author works in a higher education institution, he or she may have asked their own IT department to supply the artwork. Sometimes the detail of this arrangement is a bit vague and sub-editorial need to know if getting the artwork in hand is priority work.
- What is the status of the artwork, or perhaps photographs, line drawings, diagrams or maps that the author has supplied? Must they be returned? Production must be told. Must the illustrations be printed on glossy paper or can they be printed onto the page? It is unlikely

that you and the author have not discussed this at all, but any agreement you have reached must be conveyed to production.

- Is the book on the short side and needs bulking out? If it requires thicker paper than your company normally uses, tell production. If your book is short but your market narrow, then you need to ensure that it looks as though it is worth the high price you will have to put on it.

These are just some examples of the information that must be conveyed to your colleagues. The list is potentially very long. In essence it should contain anything that is an exception to the normal passage of a typescript through sub-editorial and production. For editors in education or other textbook publishing, or in illustrated publishing, this process is endemic to the way they work in editorial teams. They will not need to be informed in this way. They will all work on the book together.

WRITING BLURBS

Writing blurbs is a skill and it is a skill that can be learned. Granted, there are editors whose intrinsic writing ability is above average. For the rest of us it is a skill that we try to improve constantly. Many publishing houses make courses on copy writing available to their staff and if offered a place on a course, take it. If you think that blurb writing is an issue for you and your colleagues, suggest to your line manager that the company put on a dedicated blurb-writing workshop for you.

These are the basic ground rules of copy writing:

- Start and finish a blurb with a strong statement.
- Never begin a blurb with 'This book...'.
- Never misrepresent your book in the blurb, especially if you are making legal or factual claims.
- Check your blurb for incorrect grammar. Also check it to make sure it makes sense. Blurbs for some contemporary books in, for example, literary theory, have become almost incomprehensible, even to the specialist reader.
- Keep the description of the book as brief as possible. Dwell on the benefits that the book offers.
- Do not be afraid to 'sell' your book. Consumer books blurbs have to sell the book but so should specialist ones. Bring an assertive edge to your copy.

Incorporate 'puffs' from readers' reports or from reviews of an author's previous books wherever you can.

WHO ELSE IS INVOLVED?

The starting point for a good blurb, as ever, lies with the author. The author questionnaire will inevitably include a section in which the author is asked to describe the book, usually in about 250 words. Convey to authors that they are being asked essentially to write 'selling copy' for the book. If they are left with the impression that a description of the book is what is being asked for, a description is what you will get. If the angle is turned just slightly in this way you are likely to get acceptable copy from them. It is almost inevitable that it will have to be worked on to improve it but the better the raw material, the easier will be your task.

For a high-profile book, input from marketing will probably be mandatory. Indeed, in some houses, staff are employed simply to write jacket and promotion copy.

Many hard-pressed editors ask their editorial assistants to write the blurbs for them. This is in order, as long as the assistant is given plenty of guidance and as long as you thoroughly check and approve any copy provided before it moves through into production.

Remember that there are blurbs for every occasion and that a jacket blurb may not suit a catalogue. Be adaptable and bear in mind the prime function of the blurb you are writing.

FORM-FILLING

Forms are necessary. They provide comparatively simple means of conveying information. They have a kind of rough justice to them in that they ensure that all books are notionally treated equally, since the same questions have to be asked of each book. It is likely that somebody in-house has at some time made a great effort to devise forms that need to serve many purposes. From time to time some houses set up committees precisely to devise and improve their forms. Forms may differ from house to house, but you are likely to handle, at the very least, marketing, production, sub-editorial and design forms.

Sitting on committees set up to devise forms is not the most interesting job in the world to be landed with but, if we have to have forms, it is best they are devised by people who are entirely familiar with the real information requirements of a publishing house.

- Do not fill in forms using handwriting. Trying to follow handwritten forms can be heavy going, even if you are quite familiar with an editor's handwriting. In some huge publishing corporations, these forms are photocopied and sent around the world to their overseas offices. It is surprising how peculiar British handwriting looks to an American, and vice versa. You need your overseas colleagues to drum up valuable export sales for you. Don't make it difficult for them by sending them material that is just plain hard to read.

- Encourage the author to fill in author and marketing questionnaires (they may be one and the same) as fully as possible. Explain that it can be a very important factor in selling their book (see p. 99, Marketing checklist).
- Do not put useless remarks on forms such as 'please see me about this', or 'to follow'. This is a waste of time and confusing for the person on the receiving end.

Generally speaking, most editors are not naturally happy doing paperwork. They prefer working on the creative side. Publishing houses have today become more complex places, more departmentalised and international. Good-quality paperwork passing between departments in an organisation and between international offices is now vital to the smooth functioning of these companies and certainly enhances any book's chances of being promoted and marketed at least reasonably well in overseas territories. This is why it is important in all paperwork, including forms, to be clear, explicit, succinct, and to remember that anyone reading this material is not nearly as familiar with your new books as you are. For editors filling in forms with overseas colleagues in mind, remember not to be parochial.

Finally, it is perfectly permissible for a busy, over-stretched editor to ask his or her editorial assistant to do much of the form-filling and paperwork; but check it very carefully when it is finished. It is, after all, still your responsibility.

CO-PUBLICATIONS

We begin with co-publications as traditionally understood: i.e. a joint publication between two quite separate publishing houses, each publishing in a discrete territory or set of territories. These have consequences for the production process. We then move on to an arrangement which will be very familiar to those working in houses owned by large, multinational corporations: an ongoing marketing and distribution arrangement between houses in different territories, all owned by the same corporation. For the corporation, automatic distribution through its houses in different territories is seen as an important part of its global strategy.

There are implications for you in both methods.

TRADITIONAL CO-PUBLICATION DEAL

- A copy of the finished typescript will be required by the co-publishers so that they can ascertain the extent of their interest and whether they will want to buy copies from you or produce their own edition. The sooner they get to see the material on offer, the quicker they can make their decision. You certainly need to schedule all this in good time for them to join your print run.

- If they decide to buy copies, the moment that final plant costs become available, you need to formulate the complete print run, add on the costs of printing a title page with their imprint on it and similarly the extra costs of their imprinted jacket so that you can quote them a unit price.
- You need to get from the other publisher, as quickly as possible, their copy for the title page (and verso of course) and their copy for the jacket blurb if they do not wish to use yours. Send them your blurbs at an early stage!
- You need to pass to your production department full shipping instructions, which your overseas publisher will supply. In many publishing houses production departments take responsibility for shipping. It might be different in your company.
- Make sure that you send the other company a copy of the author's questionnaire. It could be useful to them.

If the other company is not buying copies from you but is using film of your typesetting, this simplifies matters enormously for you but you will need to settle on a global price for the use of the film or an offset fee based on a price per page and, again, arrange for prompt shipping overseas. Publishing houses who deal regularly with each other on co-publications tend to develop a readily understood 'going rate' for offsetting. If you are not sure of what you think you should be charging, consult your senior colleagues.

In some publishing houses it will be the foreign and subsidiary rights department which takes responsibility for co-edition deals. In which case, much of the work described will be done by someone else. At the very least, however, you will be required to liaise with the sub-rights department and you should therefore be aware of what the procedures and the requirements are.

ONGOING OVERSEAS DISTRIBUTION ARRANGEMENTS

Here another set of procedures take place which nevertheless have some elements in common with the traditional co-edition deal. The assumption is that your co-partners will, in the normal course of events, market the book in their territory (i.e. you do not have to persuade them to take the book in the first place). Companies obviously differ in their policies.

Some are plugged into comprehensive world-wide distribution; others selectively carry books from their fellow member companies. Whatever your company's arrangements are, you are likely to need to provide the following information:

- a sales letter to your colleagues setting out carefully the book's strengths, its applicability to the local market, the competition in that market which you and the author might know of, and any interesting and relevant information on the author
- a blurb that can be used not just for assessing the title but also for future promotion purposes
- an indicator of what your price and print run are likely to be so that they can begin to formulate ideas about their first stock holding and the local price

These constitute the absolute basics of this kind of international publishing co-activity. Not only do practices vary from company to company but sometimes, for particular titles, the activity can begin to resemble that for genuine co-publications. For example, your American/British office might be very excited about a new title, order 4,000 to 5,000 copies, with their own blurb on the jacket, and, what's more, will want to have a big say in the design of the jacket. In this case, they are not simply distributing the title for you, they are actively publishing the book. When they do that, you must do everything to meet their needs – but on the understanding that they will have to pay for anything that increases overall production costs.

BRIEFING DESIGNERS

Designers work on the inside and outside of books. Many editors working on textual content books tend to think that design is something solely concerned with the book's jacket.

ILLUSTRATED BOOKS

For highly illustrated books the design comes first, with the page becoming a sophisticated interrelationship between text and photographs and/or illustrations. We often think of the highly illustrated book as a product of general publishing – cookery books, gardening books, art books, and so on. However, educational books and medical books, for example, are just as carefully designed and illustrated. Expert colleagues in production come into their own in this kind of work but the editor must play a key role in the design team. The team can sometimes consist of editor, author, designer, photographer, illustrator, picture researchers, and even the agent.

The editor must, with the author (and probably marketing and production colleagues) go through every illustration in the book and the text to which it is tied. Agreement is needed for the captions, the keys (if there are any), the colours, the notes and the size of an illustration in relation to the text. Everyone must be involved and prepared to work with a meticulous attention to detail.

JACKET DESIGN

If you seldom work on illustrated books, then your most frequent point of contact with designers will be over the book's jacket. Again, practices differ from one type of publishing category to another and from one house to another.

- You may work in a publishing house where you have no influence or input in the process – where perhaps marketing colleagues brief design on the jacket. In such houses the editor's task is simply to relay back to design whether the author likes the jacket or not and, unhappily, the editor can get caught uncomfortably in the middle when the author really doesn't like the jacket and wants it changed.
- In consumer books publishing it is not uncommon for authors' agents to have a clause written into the contract that states that the author must approve the jacket design. If the author is important to you, then this is something you have to live with even when the author rejects jacket design after jacket design before you come up with something acceptable. It is expensive and time-consuming but it might be the price of keeping the author on your list.
- Before embarking on the design of a new book from such an author, at the very least try to recall what it was about the jacket of the previous book which they liked, and the kind of thing they rejected. With luck it is possible to avoid the obvious pitfalls, but this process is rather hit or miss and the author may be rejecting designs for reasons that have nothing to do with design at all. He or she might subconsciously feel that the design process is something that has to be gone through several times before the best can emerge.

If it is your job to brief the jacket designer – at the very least aided by your marketing colleagues – it is necessary to bear the following in mind.

DESIGN CHECKLIST

- The editor's fundamental job is to convey to the designer the character of the book, to explain some of the basic 'messages' that are implicit in it, the kinds of 'signals' that the jacket must give off in order to attract the audience to which it is aimed: should it be friendly and approachable or austere, should it be plain and classic or busy and frenetic? A good analogy to bear in mind when trying to convey the principles of briefing jacket design is that you are choosing the clothes to suit the book: how should it be dressed?

- Remember, always keep it simple. No book jacket design can hope to cover all the ideas or information contained in a book. Simple design is still effective design.
- Never pass entire responsibility over to the designer. Too often editors tell designers that they are 'just hopeless at this sort of thing' and ask the designer to go away and come up with something. Unless you are very lucky, the designer is quite likely to come up with designs that do not suit the book and everyone's time has been wasted. This is also an expensive business to waste time and money on. Designers' fees have to be paid and when paying for rejected design (rejected through no fault of the designer often), then the jacket is likely to cost twice what it should!
- Resist the temptation to ask for a famous painting or photograph for the jacket illustration, or for four colours, when something rather more modest is not only appropriate but also desirable. High-level specialist books are bought for their content, not for the jacket. In this kind of publishing, books are not impulse buys. Spending a lot on illustration and design here is wasting valuable money. The reverse is certainly true for fiction publishing.
- Do not forget that the design of the spine is equally important. A well-designed spine stands out from others on the bookshop shelves and should be easily readable.
- Never allow the author to take a hand in the jacket design unless he or she is professionally qualified to do so. Jacket design is specialist design and requires particular skills. A general rule of thumb is that the more the author wants to design the jacket, the less able is he or she to do just that. Jacket design sometimes brings out the worst kind of interfering tendencies in authors, because it can take on enormous symbolic value.

For example, the closer authors come to publication day, the more anxious they tend to get about whether the book will be received and sell well. This is perfectly understandable and natural. For authors who find it almost impossible to handle their anxiety, the sight of a jacket proof and a design they find not to their liking is enough to trigger off waves of anger and resentment. The first time editors encounter this, they are simply baffled and terribly disconcerted by the ferocity of the reaction, until they realise that the jacket has provided the author with a wonderfully handy dumping ground for all the feelings of anxiety and inadequacy that simply cannot be acknowledged at the time.

- Always remember that the book is the author's, not yours, and it would be unfortunate to inflict on him or her a design that he or she will hate for ever more. Far better to have an author who looks at the book with happy approval than one who grinds his or her teeth and thoroughly resents you. They may not want to publish with you again.

  The wisest thing is to talk to the author before the design stage about what sort of design they would be happy with. Make it absolutely clear if there are real budgetary considerations that there is not endless cash to spend on something lavish. Get some sort of feel for how the author sees it, what he or she thinks the messages should be.

  Having given the author permission to contribute, one then often finds that he or she has very little to say but feels far happier for having been asked. Frequently they will say quite mundane things like, 'Well, I would prefer if you didn't use red', or 'Please don't use a black-and-white photo', or 'I hate block lettering'. You can easily deal with this.

- If you do find that you are dealing with an author who has become impossible over this issue, remember that the vast majority of contracts give you the sole right to decide over production matters. You might very well have to resort to the contract and do not be afraid to do so if all attempts to reconcile the author have failed. It is a risk because you might have a resentful and angry author for ever. On the other hand, you might be surprised to have a phone call from that same author, sometime later, saying that he or she is beginning to like the jacket after all. This does happen.

- Designers do, with all the careful briefing in the world, still come up with lousy jackets. Do not be afraid to say so and reject them. In particular, if you are presented with a bad design, resist the temptation to tinker with it. You are probably prolonging the agony. Reject it straight away and ask the designer to come up with something fresh. Or ask another designer to work on the jacket.

Never forget that design is a subjective business. If colleagues in editorial, marketing and sales are all involved in the approval of a jacket, there is a strong chance that disagreement will emerge from time to time. Design by uneasy consensus will not work. It is better to have a jacket agreed on by a majority vote than one that tries to be all things to everyone involved.

LIAISON WITH MARKETING

Marketing is a subject in its own right. What is attempted here is a hit list of essentials – those ideas, information, the approach to adopt – when you talk to your marketing colleagues about how they are going to sell your book.

Start with this in mind. It may not be glaringly obvious to anyone else but you that the book you are about to launch on the world is just wonderful. It is so easy, especially when relatively inexperienced, to assume that everyone else has been able to spot the book's merits, the potential market, and so on. You might have become intimate with it; your colleagues haven't. If you are publishing consistently successful authors such as Stephen King, Philip Pullman, Jilly Cooper, P. D. James or Joanna Trollope, then, yes, there are few things that need to be explained.

The majority of authors are not automatic best sellers. It is necessary to explain carefully to your colleagues in marketing why they might have a potential success on their hands. That is particularly the case in specialist publishing where the subject matter of a new book is seldom what lay readers (i.e. your colleagues) are likely to be expert in. In consumer books non-fiction publishing, where the editor is closer to the author's world through frequent contact with him or her, an editor can come up with ideas that can lift a marketing campaign.

MARKETING CHECKLIST

1 Ensure that the author has filled in the author's questionnaire fully and constructively. It is your job to convey to the author the importance of this document to the marketing department. The following must be explained:

   (a) You already have a great deal of market intelligence and experience in-house but the author is closer to the readership and might have additional information which will be valuable.

   (b) The author should be explicit when giving information. Vague instructions or references will not help.

   (c) When giving names of individuals to receive copies, the author should give addresses too.

   (d) Advertising spend is not limitless and the author should prioritise publications where advertisements would help sales.

   (e) Lists for review copies should appear in order of importance. If the author has connections that could lead to reviews, these should be specified fully.

   (f) Full details of courses, and teaching, professional training or leisure association applicability should be given, including information on where lists for direct marketing can be obtained.

(g) Authors should always provide international information (including possible translation interest) wherever they can.

Some authors do not like filling in questionnaires and when they do, make no effort or return something that is sloppy. Persist, and if you are ever told, 'Well, I've written the book and you should know how to market it', tell the author this is going to be the best opportunity he or she is likely to get to influence the way in which the marketing is done. That marketing has to be planned ahead and that it will be pointless the author complaining after publication. It is advisable to get the questionnaire delivered with the typescript, so that if you do encounter this problem, it can be tackled at an early stage.

2 Do your homework properly by providing your colleagues with:
   (a) the sales records of the author's previous books;
   (b) full details of books that are in print or in preparation which might compete with this title;
   (c) the details of the course work for which it is designed, if the book is aimed at some part of the education market.

If you are also co-publishing with overseas colleagues, remember to provide them with as much as you can of this kind of information.

3 Be prepared to bombard your colleagues with information. When they draw up specific marketing and sales plans, they will extract what is relevant and effective from what is simply nice and interesting to know. Indeed, a good marketeer will sometimes find a real nugget of marketing relevance out of what you might have thought was of second-rank importance.

4 Always talk about the book in terms of the benefits to the reader that come from buying it. By specifying the benefits, you give colleagues the springboard from which they launch their marketing plans and ideas.

5 Always present books positively. It is unreasonable to expect marketing to become enthusiastic and energised over a book presented to them in a diffident fashion.

6 Marketing is intrinsically looking for simple but telling messages about a book. Always ensure that the messages are correct. Books can sometimes be quite unwittingly misrepresented.

7 In some of the bigger publishing houses marketing has become systematised and rationalised just like everything else. Remember that an interesting twist or angle on the marketing approach might just make the difference between good and indifferent sales, and that you might be the one to make the difference. Standardised marketing is likely to lead to rather standardised sales.

8 Highlight direct marketing and telemarketing potential through special sales to lists of book buyers, memberships of clubs, professional groups or associations, including bulk sales.

PROMOTION CHECKLIST

Depending on how the scheduling in your house runs, some time ahead of publication day you will be shown a promotion plan for the book and if you haven't been, make sure to obtain one. Examine it carefully to make sure that everything has been covered:

- review lists
- advertisements
- complimentary copies for influential people
- display copies for conferences
- inspection copies for teachers, lecturers, trainers
- point-of-sale material
- author signings (if appropriate)
- launch party (if appropriate)
- other bookshop events
- public relations activity
- direct marketing
- shelf liners
- posters – adshel (bus stop adverts) and underground
- television and radio appearances and special programmes
- website features
- when appropriate, mailings to reading groups if your house has established links with them

SALES CONFERENCES

Marketing and sales colleagues would probably scarcely credit the anxiety that most editors go through when they have to 'perform' at a sales conference. The word perform is used quite deliberately because your presentation should be a performance. You have an audience and you need an effective 'script' to go with it. Preparation is almost everything.

Most people are quite naturally nervous when they have to face an audience. The heightened edge for editors is that what they are responsible for – the book, the commercial judgement that backs it – has come from them and for just a few moments, all that is exposed. The simple process of trying to find the right words to convey the right messages, and of saying them aloud, is quite frightening. Fear can remain with editors even when very experienced. Draining as it is, it is probably a good thing: it keeps editors on their toes and is likely to lead to a better performance than if they feel complacent and over-confident. Practice will make you, if not perfect, altogether more effective. If your company makes training days in effective presentation available to its editors, make sure you take the opportunity to get some.

PRESENTATION CHECKLIST

- Keep your presentation succinct. Do not ramble on, especially with an endless description of the book. There is nothing sales reps dread more, for example, than the detailed plot of a novel laid out for them.
- This is the one time when you must present the benefits of purchasing this book rather than dwelling on its excellent qualities in isolation. Spell out clearly to the reps what translates this book into a 'must have'.
- If you can, give the reps a 'hook' on which they can hang the book. Do you have an interesting or amusing story that flows from it – it could concern the author, for example? You are looking for something that will cause the book to be lodged quite firmly in the reps' minds. They may have to listen to 20 editors or more presenting altogether several hundred books.
- Be sure to point out any events taking place that might help provide publicity for a book. For example, if the author is going to give a special lecture somewhere, make sure the regional rep knows. Or perhaps on publication day, the author is publishing in a national newspaper an article that links in with this book and will heighten interest in it. Remember that the reps are always looking for ammunition to take into bookshops when they are trying to sell in stock.
- Never oversell a title to your reps. Next time you stand up in front of them exaggerating the qualities of a book, they will be less inclined to believe you. Be honest. It is perfectly in order to say, 'This is mundane, bread and butter stuff, but it is exactly what students want for their course on . . .'. Prioritise your titles: some are more important than others.
- Look cheerful or, at the very least, positive and confident.
- Practise your presentation over and over again in private so that by the time you stand up in front of the sales conference, you have honed your script and you practically know it off by heart. And always say your presentation aloud beforehand so that you can hear how your words sound. Words said in the head and words said out loud are quite different. Try doing it in front of the mirror!
- Use visual aids to engage the audience's interest – jacket designs, illustrations from the book, photographs or attractively presented statistics. Anything that will help get your points across.
- Get to know the sales team and personalise your presentation to involve them in your enthusiasm. Remember the territories they cover,

and above all, remember their names. Indeed, use their names if a book is going to be of direct appeal to a particular territory. 'Here's one for you, Tom!' If Tom has been snoozing up until then (which is not unknown at sales conferences), he is going to sit up and listen from there on in. Congratulate them on past successes with similar titles.

- After the conference, get feedback on your presentation from your colleagues. Sales and marketing colleagues are most likely to give you honest answers.

Always resolve to do better at your next sales conference.

If your company does not include interactive sessions at its sales conferences, during which reps are encouraged to comment on sales figures and jacket designs, for example, suggest it to your sales manager. These sessions can produce quite scathing comments, but they are usually highly instructive.

Finally, if you only meet your reps at sales conferences and at times feel bewildered or disappointed at their reactions to new books, try spending time on the road with one or two of them. Most editors have no idea what it is like to sell new titles into the shops. This really is the sharp end of publishing and a few days' exposure to it will give an editor a far keener idea of how their product has to compete in the market place.

INVOLVING THE AUTHOR

The author has provided a questionnaire, which you will have exhorted him or her to fill in as fully as possible. It will be examined in great detail, by marketing colleagues both in the domestic and overseas markets, to generate marketing activities and ideas. But in addition to all that, there is the author in person

It's good to show off some authors; others should be kept hidden. The most successful authors are not always the best presenters of their own material, but the two usually coincide. They are good at presenting and talking about their material because they are essentially good communicators. Now you can put an author to several good uses.

Only the very famous and successful are candidates for bookshop signings because the bookshops are, perfectly understandably, only interested in having their shops used for signing events that are going to sell large numbers of books on the day. Signings are complicated, need a great deal of organisation and entirely disrupt the rest of the bookshop business while they are going on.

Equally, only the famous and successful are likely to be invited on television chat shows to be interviewed on the occasion of the publication of their book.

On the other hand, much less glamorous books and authors make ideal material for radio and television discussion programmes. Until you have had direct dealings with the other media (including newspapers), it is difficult to understand just how much those media feed off books as a resource for entertainment and information. The media need feeding every day and books provide an ideal source for stories and features. A judicious choice of author and book on the part of the editor working in conjunction with a PR manager, who knows how to approach the media, can result in some nice publicity bonuses. In the case of consumer books, this publicity is essential.

You can also consider using an author at the sales conference. Reps do like to meet a real, live author. A good presentation from a lively and entertaining author can transform a routine sales conference into a sense of occasion. Again, the author has to be chosen carefully. Everyone must understand what they aim to achieve by bringing the author in and, most importantly, you must brief your author very carefully about how long you want them to talk for, what essentially you want them to cover, and some guidance about how to 'pitch' the presentation.

Everyone has apocryphal stories about authors who were blind drunk, who insulted the publishers, who told dirty jokes, who rambled on and on. The staff at one publisher's conference were once 'entertained' by a man who had written a book about sea shanties. He sang for about an hour and a half, by which time the audience was desperate for relief.

Author appearances are essential at consumer books sales conferences. Choosing the right one is part and parcel of the planning ahead. Humour writers are favourites because they make everyone laugh and feel more relaxed. Although the choice of author to be invited usually lies with the publishing and marketing directors, if you think you have an author who can excel on such an occasion, make sure his or her name goes forward for consideration.

PUBLICATION DAY

With all the grand plans that are being formulated for publication day and the run-up to it, it is very easy to forget to do the small things that can make a difference. Publication day is a big event, even for the most experienced author.

* Signal to the author that you are aware of the day and its signifi-
  cance. A note or a telephone call is a good enough gesture. If the
  author is of colossal importance to your house, you will probably

want to mark the occasion with flowers or a very good lunch or dinner. These events are redolent of the cliché but they can still have their effect.

- Make sure also that the author receives the complimentary copies by publication day. It is good policy to send the author the very first copy of the book to reach you from the printer, with a promise that the rest of the complimentary copies will be on their way as soon as the bulk of the stock is in. That first copy (hot from the press) is much appreciated.

- Check with the sales manager if sales have been made into the author's local bookshop and that the stock is there by publication day. The author is bound to go looking for the book. Some years ago an author came to London for a few days' holiday with his wife during the week of publication. He went into Foyles bookshop in central London and found a large pile of his books on one of the main display tables on the ground floor. He was so delighted that when he rang the editor later that day, he seemed implicitly to feel that somehow or other the editor had arranged it. The editor explained that the Central London rep had simply done a good job but also enjoyed the author's great pleasure. That was his first book but it established a strong link between both of them that lasted many years.

- After publication day is over, make it a discipline to send your author (1) reviews (or maybe your marketing department does this automatically) and (2) sales figures on a regular basis. They might get to see the bulk of the reviews anyway but they will have very little idea of how sales are going. Some authors of course do like to check at their local bookshops whether the stock has been sold and if there is more on order, and that gives them some sense of how the book is selling, but it is only a partial picture.

  It is never easy to have to confront a disappointed author with miserable reviews and even more unsatisfactory sales but you might as well get on with supplying them, because they are inevitably going to ask you for them. You can carry on sending copies of reviews until they have dried up. Sales information can be discontinued once the author has started receiving the sales statements that come with royalty payments.

- Authors also need to be advised promptly about the sales of book club rights or foreign language editions. They also need to be advised when, sadly, their books are put out of print or remaindered. For specialist publishers this bad news is not likely to be imparted for several years. For consumer books publishers, alas, it can be within a year of publication.

DEALING WITH INAPPROPRIATE BEHAVIOUR

AUTHOR INTRUSION

The author's ego manifests itself in many ways. The author with the large but confident ego is likely to give you very little trouble. The author with the anxious ego is something else and authors whose anxiety is just plain out of control spell trouble. They are likely to make demands on you and your house that are inappropriate. The most common centre around promotion and marketing.

- Typically an author imagines that the budget for promoting and marketing a book is bottomless. The more money is spent telling the world how good a book is, the thinking goes, the more likely sales are to increase. The expenditure is therefore justified. Unfortunately, there are very few books published for which the demand is completely elastic.
- Specialist books, in particular, have an inelastic market. There are only so many sociologists in Britain, or elsewhere, who want the last word on postmodernism on their desks and by and large your marketing colleagues know how to reach them and how much it will cost. Any expenditure over above that is wasted expenditure.
- Consumer books, of course, have a much more elastic market and here you are more likely to encounter authors demanding a yet bigger marketing spend. Marshall your arguments around examples of a typical spend for this sort of book and give sales figures for successful books which did have a comparable promotion budget. In this way the author is reminded that the book does have to succeed on its own merits in the end, just like all other books.
- Guard therefore against agreeing that your company will spend more on promotion and marketing than you know can be justified by the sales. Advertising and author tours in particular fall into this category, and so do lavish launch parties. Many books get advertised, even if in a quite limited way; some extremely successful authors are asked to tour bookshops and attend other events; even low-key books can have their publication day marked by a quiet party for the author.
- All this is part and parcel of the promotion and marketing plan which is drawn up for any book. Discard anything from the author that is overblown and will lead to wasted expenditure. It will be your job to say 'no' but you must and explain why. Never agree to anything exceptional of this sort before talking to your marketing colleagues first. And never, under pressure from an author, invent marketing

plans 'on the hoof'. Your input into the plans is vital, and so is the author's, but at the end of the day, responsibility for marketing lies with your marketing colleagues and you should never attempt to make marketing plans that exclude them. Clear things with marketing first, however much you might be in awe or frightened of, or even in thrall to, the author. Most books benefit from a certain amount of free publicity anyway: reviews, a mention in a feature article or on a radio programme. It can come up quite unexpectedly sometimes.

AUTHOR ANXIETY

Quite common are the sorts of difficulties which arise when an author's perfectly understandable anxieties roar out of control. Writing and publishing a book is a stressful thing. But so are many other things in life and anyone who experiences and has to deal with their own stress knows they have to cope without dumping it on other people. Not everyone can do this and emotionally immature adults are particularly bad at managing their stress. Your work as an editor is bound to bring you into contact with examples of this sort. What is likely to happen?

- You will become the source of blame. You are the first and most important contact at the publishing house and therefore can take the blame for schedules, design, marketing, sales, anything.
- Demands will be made of you – marketing demands have just been mentioned. Time is often the most common: daily phone calls with questions and more questions; rambling conversations; long letters that turn into essays about how the book should be published. Sometimes you discover that your colleagues in sub-editorial or marketing are also being bullied behind your back. Even after publication day phone calls and letters still continue with the same intensity. This is all part of the same phenomenon: 'Mine is the only book you are publishing this year.'
- When this is encountered, gently find ways of reminding the author that there are other authors, just like him or her, waiting to be published by you. If you are busy, say that you are busy. Put their books in the context of the rest of the work to be done. If this kind of author gains the impression that you are always there any day and any time – he or she will become overwhelming because you will never be able to do enough to assuage his or her anxieties. Yours is a professional relationship after all.
- Beware also of authors who might try to play you off against other members of your team. This does happen and you might not even

know it is going on until demands become critical. You must ensure, therefore, that everyone in your team is exchanging information about approaches the author might have made about anything from sub-editorial matters to marketing plans.

However, to be scrupulously fair to the author, always ask yourself, am I giving this author all the information he or she needs, and at the right time, or am I continually putting him or her in the position of having to ask for it? If it is the latter, then make life easier for yourself by properly informing them and properly taking their advice.

YOUR OWN ANXIETY!

Remember that you might find being an editor difficult at times too and that your own behaviour might leave something to be desired. There are many ways in which an editor mishandles his or her own stress but in the period between delivery date and publication day this misman-agement commonly takes two forms:

- The first might be termed 'letting go', and letting go too early. As mentioned before, the typescript will pass through other hands in your house and other expertises come into play. It is very tempting simply to pass it all on, with some sense of relief. But you chose to publish it, convinced your colleagues that it should be published, and have been nurturing the book and the author. Your personal invest-ment has been far too expensive to throw away now. You must oversee that book every step up to and beyond publication day to make quite sure that the best is done by it.
- The second must be called just plain 'running away'. Editors do run away from their books because they cannot bear the anxiety and uncer-tainty surrounding their publication. Running away manifests itself in the same way as 'letting go': you keep handing on responsibility to someone else. Does it matter therefore if a distinction is drawn between the two, since the effect is the same? It does, because if you are a self-imposed victim of the latter, you have a lot more work to do on yourself if you are going to avoid damaging your books and probably your colleagues too. Running away will never solve the problems that being an editor poses and if you refuse to deal with those problems, perhaps you shouldn't be an editor.

CASE STUDIES

1   An academic editor was very pleased to have persuaded a most distinguished writer to offer the publishing house her latest book. She already
had a handful of titles in print. The author had a reputation for being
extraordinarily clever, articulate and situated at the apex of the contemporary cultural milieu. She was, to sum it up, a catch.

   The editor became rather nervous when it came to briefing the jacket
designer. He ached to offer the author a jacket that was as 'cutting
edge' as she was. The best designer (freelancer) was therefore
summoned and briefed by the editor. The first designs disappointed
the editor, and the designer was despatched to try again. The second
designs also disappointed. By now, both the editor and the designer
were becoming tense. The head of design and the editor decided to
give the job to another freelancer. He produced two extremely disappointing designs and was also 'let go'. By now, it was clear to everyone
around that the editor no longer knew what he wanted, if he ever had.
A third designer produced designs that were sent to the author for
approval. She hated them. The editor was mortified by her reaction.
Back to the drawing-board! The book was now in extreme danger of
being delayed. What is more, three lots of design fees had already
been paid, and still there was no design in sight.

   An observant in-house designer, by now bemused by what was going
on, as indeed was everyone else, decided to have a bash at the jacket
himself. He produced a plain, typographical jacket that had some
elegance and showed it to the editor. In exhaustion, the editor sent it
to the author. She loved it. It was, she said, the kind of design she
was hoping they would come up with.

QUESTION

Where did this situation start to go wrong and why? If you had been
the editor, how would you have handled the author? How would you
have stopped the process of design turning into such a protracted
problem? Do you think that high-profile authors are difficult to deal with
on such matters?

2   A consumer books editor running a list for readers with special interests contracted a book from an author who had previously published only with large, international consumer books publishers. The author had an agent, who had put a lot of pressure on the editor to get the book signed. The author lived abroad. Suddenly she announced she was flying to London to be there to coincide with the publication of her book. Her schedule was unknown. Basically, she had given her editor about two days' notice that she was on her way.

Suddenly she turned up at the editor's office and clearly expected everyone to clear the decks to deal with her. In the course of the meeting, the author indicated strongly that she was expecting a launch party, a book-signing session and thought it was worthwhile attending some literary events around the country, supported by a sales and promotion team. At the first indications of surprise, followed by polite expressions of resistance on the part of the editor, the author ranted and raved, rang her agent within the presence of the editor and chewed him up for putting her in the hands of such incompetent people. She stormed out declaring she would arrange her own PR activities using her friends whom she knew would help her out. A list of events, and what was required of the publisher, turned up after a couple of days. For about a week, the editor and colleagues from marketing spent their time running around the country carrying boxes of the author's new book from one rather disappointing event to another.

QUESTION

Here we have a genuine example of the author as monster. But she was not entirely at fault. Why was she not entirely at fault?

Strategic and financial aspects of list building   6

In this chapter we will be looking at list building:

- as a complement to the rest of your publishing
- to seize a market opportunity
- to create diversity through product and revenue
- to meet the objectives of backlist or frontlist publishing
- to increase or control market share
- allied to marketing resources
- with its implications for costs, investment and cash flow
- and problem areas

LIST BUILDING

Starting a list from scratch is something of a rarity. It most commonly happens, of course, when a new publishing house is founded. However, entrepreneurs setting up in publishing often buy lists from other publishers so that they have titles to sell the moment they open up for business. If these lists are for sale, it might be concluded, they are probably not very successful ones. Possibly, but often they are for sale because the seller has developed his or her publishing house in directions that no longer fit the list that is up for sale; or did not have the resources to sell the titles to maximum effect. In any case, *caveat emptor* operates as much in publishing as elsewhere. The buyer must ask some searching questions about what is for sale before deciding to go ahead and take the risk or not.

More commonly, a new list will be started in an established house where there are at least several other strands of publishing in existence. It is likely that the new list will bear some relation to the lists that the publisher already holds. To launch something completely different from the publishing sector already occupied is unusual and, when that happens, it is likely that the publisher probably has some long-term plan for diversification, has done the research – in the broadest sense – that is necessary before swinging slowly off in a new direction.

The publisher will also have done the financial homework fairly thoroughly to make sure that any extra resources which will be needed can be found and that the return on investment will be at least adequate. Good examples of dramatic diversification would be a consumer books house that decides to enter education publishing, or a medical publisher that decides to enter business publishing. It seems unlikely, but it does happen. Chapman & Hall began in the nineteenth century as a literary publishing house which published, among others, Charles Dickens. In the twentieth century it became one of the most distinguished STM publishers in the English-speaking world. Its transformation took place in a comparatively short period of time in the 1940s.

Such radical transformations are rare. They are rare because they mean that the house has to acquire a whole new area of knowledge about subject, reader, buyer and market. Such sets of knowledge usually take years to build up. Imagine if one day, after struggling to reach some sort of reasonable proficiency in publishing novels, you were suddenly asked to publish chemistry textbooks. It might seem easier to move from chemistry to novels, since we can all read novels and have some sense of judgement about them, but it's not.

CONSOLIDATION OF EXPERTISE

The point is that proficiency and expertise in publishing lie in many spheres – production, marketing and promotion, sales and design (not just editorial) – and a move into a completely different direction would require another set of skills appropriate to that direction. Most pertinently, marketing structures and operations have been developed to sell a particular kind of book and, indeed, the book trade understands that and familiarises itself with the product and develops its own awareness in relation to it. A bookshop manager recognises a Faber book, for example, and has a certain level of expectation about it. Likewise a Cape book or a Routledge book. That level of expectation, unless it is a negative one, is valuable to the publisher. The publisher does not have to fight for recognition in the market. So, disturb that at your peril.

Most commonly, a specialist publisher will diversify into another specialist list, or a consumer books publisher might move from adult fiction and non-fiction into children's publishing. There is a specific expertise needed for all those areas but, at the very least, the publisher is not trying to mount the enormous hurdle that lies between specialist and consumer books publishing.

WHY START A NEW LIST?

Variety is the spice of life and nowhere more so than in publishing. However, if you are at the top of the tree in humanities publishing, is it strictly necessary to move into the social sciences or into professional publishing? It is terribly tempting to want to try something new, especially if you can see another publisher being rather successful in it, but it is most advisable that the new does bear some relation to what you are already doing.

A good idea is one thing; the realisation of it is something else. When you decide to go down a new road, there are many things you must consider carefully before being convinced that a new development can be a successful one. Below are the main issues you should be looking at.

OPPORTUNITY

Very occasionally a highly perceptive editor will, through a combination of market research plus a simple but telling ability to look into the future and guess where a trend might develop, spot a brand new area about to open up and where all evidence suggests that no other publisher has spotted it. This is the ideal, and it is a rare situation to be immediately at the forefront of something which is taking off and to have no competition to deal with. If the list is successful, that publishing house will soon be joined by others but, for the moment anyway, they have a head start. Virago, certainly in consumer books publishing, is a very good example of a feminist house that took the risk of starting a new genre of books in the 1970s. Many competitors joined them later.

ADDING VALUE

A publisher can start a list or even develop one that he or she already has but add on a distinctive characteristic which will give it advantage in the market-place; for example, by changing the format or the pricing. Some paperback houses in the 1980s introduced 'B' format paperbacks. Bigger than the conventional paperback, they were more elegantly printed and more securely bound. Here publishers recognised that there was a paperback buyer who was prepared to pay a little more for a paperback, usually when it was considered to be 'serious literature'. Other examples would be quite literally adding on a computer disk, or a workbook of exercises, or maps. Or one might do what Dorling

Kindersley did and add huge value to their books by designing and illustrating them in an exceptionally brilliant way which was much admired, and now copied.

DIVERSIFICATION

As in many manufacturing industries, any supplier who becomes dependent on a relatively small range of goods becomes vulnerable. If one of those lines goes through bad times, it puts that much more strain on the others to perform well. A sensible planner in a publishing office will from time to time decide that perhaps it is just as well to put eggs in several baskets and diversify.

MANAGING REVENUES

If you are in the business of producing big books – dictionaries, encyclopaedias, standard reference works, all of which are expensive and lengthy in their preparation – you might want to introduce a new strand of publishing where books are realised quickly and less expensively, thereby injecting some quick cash into your revenues. Conversely, having been dependent on books with a short publication cycle and inevitably not very highly priced, you might want to add some ballast to your revenues by introducing what is often known as the 'door stopper': a big book that, although expensive to produce, can command very high prices.

FRONTLIST VERSUS BACKLIST

If a publisher's list mostly contains the sort of book that goes immediately out of print when stocks are sold out, then you are dependent on frontlist sales and are probably a consumer books publisher, and a mass market paperback publisher at that. For the specialist publishers, the situation is reversed. They have books that stay in print for five years or more. There are up- and down-sides for both types. For the consumer books publisher, crudely put, revenues come in quickly but marketing costs are high. For the specialist, cash comes in very slowly and can take up to a year before it has real impact, but marketing costs are lower over the entire publishing life of a book which can go on steadily selling when its consumer cousins have long been forgotten.

· While this area has clear connections with the control of revenue flows just mentioned above, backlist versus frontlist has distinct implications for the kind of book that gets commissioned. It is pointless saying that you want to create a backlist if you do not commission the kind of book that does have real staying power. One of the reasons why Penguin has been so successful over the years is that although it is a mass market paperback publisher, it has a brilliant backlist. The backlist is looked at in greater detail in the following chapter.

DOMINATING THE MARKET

If you hold the high ground in your particular field, it might be worthwhile introducing new publishing strands simply to keep the competition out. In order to smother any competitor who has a toehold in your field, one approach is to introduce competitive lists just to emphasise your predominance in this field. Perhaps you are a huge and immensely successful law publisher whose books are essentially reference books for lawyers and barristers in practice and one day you realise that a smaller competitor has just started publishing books for law students. While this market is not as lucrative as the professional one, it might be wise to enter it since the textbook publisher might become rich enough to provide a challenge, by starting professional reference publishing. There is also a more intangible side to this. It pays to be seen to have a finger in every pie. If you are seen as the established publisher in a particular field, then every good author will be drawn to publish with you.

SIZE AND FOCUS OF THE LIST

The truth of the matter is that list building can be as haphazard and as dependent on serendipity as anything else in publishing. Publishing is rarely a scientific process. The list is more likely to be successful if the editor does have a reasonably formed idea of how big that new list is going to be and what its focus is. It is necessary to have confidence that there will be sufficient books available for publication every year. Is there 'pace' in this market? Are there authors out there writing books? It would be foolish, for example, to launch a new list in numismatics believing you can guarantee 30 new books a year. Numismatics books are rare books and you are unlikely to reach your target. On the other hand, there seems to be no shortage of cookery writers or first novelists.

MARKET RESEARCH

You will need to show through market research that there are going to be sufficient numbers of books available in, at the very least, the next few years. This is to pay for the very considerable editorial and marketing work that is going to be required to make the newly launched list a success. To go back to the numismatics books for one moment, it might very well be worthwhile having such a list. To be sure, not many get written because it is such a specialist field but, when published, they command exceptionally high prices and the small band of numismatics experts around the world will in all probability want them. The list could be small but quite secure and very profitable.

You need to check the obvious: that there are readers for these books. There are many ways of doing this, which have been mentioned earlier (pages 22–4). Be careful when there are few statistics for you to consult. For example, when publishers started signing up their first women's studies books in the early 1970s, there were only five higher education institutions in Britain that had any kind of women's studies programme. There were no books on the publishers' backlists to help gauge what the sales might be. However, common sense said that since half the social science students in this country were female, there would be a sizeable market for the right kind of book.

Focus is important: who will these books be aimed at and what purpose will they serve? A list that is an assortment of books which seem to bear no relation to each other is going to be difficult to market. Successful marketing in publishing is built around the principle of having a 'family' of books which can be promoted and sold across the board to a fairly coherent readership. If the list is fragmented, the marketing department has to start from scratch for every book. This is inefficient and also gives mixed messages to the market-place – authors, readers, agents and booksellers.

MARKETING FACTORS

The unusual case of a specialist publisher moving into consumer books publishing or vice versa is rare, but sometimes publishers are tempted to nibble around the edges of another type of publishing. Every day editors are offered books which, whilst not strictly speaking pertinent to their lists, are in some way loosely related. For example, if you already have successful books on alcoholism or depression, but written at a high level of theory or practice, it is quite tempting to accept one that could be successful on an even broader level, but in the right hands. 'Horses for courses' is a salutary phrase to keep in mind when tempted by something just outside one's area of expertise.

Specialist publishers have marketing, sales and promotion departments set up to sell specialist books. They are good at doing just that. They have different promotion material, selling cycles, discounts, pricing structures, publicity machines and point-of-sale material from consumer books publishers. A trade book suddenly introduced into a specialist system immediately throws it off balance. The editorial and marketing expertise needed to give the book the full consumer treatment is not likely to be found in a specialist house.

Such books fail in comparison with what a fully blown consumer books publisher might achieve. Disappointment all round is the likeliest outcome, both for publisher and author. Remember, it is one thing to decide to publish a book; another to understand that you have the sales and marketing machine to sell it to its maximum potential. Similarly, there are essentially specialist authors who have been enticed by the glamour of being on a consumer books publishing list, only to feel angry and hurt at the eventual realisation that the publisher is not a backlist publisher and that his or her book is out of print a year or so after publication.

YOUR COMPETITORS

Since you don't have a list of your own to analyse, look at your competitors' lists.

- Analyse their strengths and weaknesses. Useful information can be drawn from their catalogues regarding formats and prices, their stated readerships, whether their titles are at the 'cutting edge', whether there are gaps, and so on.
- If you make friends with editors in any of these houses (which is quite likely), you may be able to glean sales figures from them. Otherwise industry-wide sales figures, such as those gathered by Neilsen Bookscan, are available for you to analyse. But beware the 'friendly' rival. Some competitors see fledgling editors as 'rich pickings' – the source of information they might want to take off you.
- Neither is there anything to prevent your approaching their authors when you are in the process of marshalling opinions.
- Remember to look at the publication dates of their books and see if their output has been rising or diminishing over time, and what conclusion you can draw from that.

Here you are putting yourself through the process of finding out what the competition does and if you can do it as well, or better, or differently.

COST FACTORS

Does this list have cost implications that are different from those with which you are familiar? A new list in architecture, art, history or sport will require illustrations. Some may be illustrated in full colour, some may require the use of plates. Such books are expensive to produce and it is vital to establish that print runs, and therefore prices, are going to cover the cost of investment and produce the desired profit.

AVAILABILITY OF INVESTMENT

Consider the question of investment itself. Many large publishing corporations have comparatively large investment budgets available to develop expensive new products. For a small or medium-size independent publisher, the arrival of a new list with high production values and costs could have very severe repercussions for cash flow. A list that will require exceptional investment should certainly be referred up to the company's management for comment.

Even if the list conforms in investment terms (on an individual book basis) to the rest of your publishing, if it is going to produce high-volume output – in terms of the number of books published – that will also have budgetary implications which need to be worked through.

At the other extreme it may be possible to start a list whose production costs are relatively low. Scholarly publishers, for example, are sometimes offered books that come with subventions (usually from institutions) to put against the cost of production. Typically such books are non-commercial in their appeal and their publication is desirable purely on scholarly grounds. In this case, the 'author' recognises that the books represent a commercial risk and is offering to share in the investment for the good of scholarship. This is a worthwhile departure for the publisher as long as that publisher does not see the subsidy as 'easy money' and becomes careless about the books. If printed and priced sensibly, they run few risks, need relatively small promotion budgets and can enhance that publisher's reputation as a serious publisher.

Similarly, in consumer books publishing, sponsored books come with subsidies which can make a huge contribution to production costs. Here you need to be quite clear about several issues. First, that there will be a genuine market for the book; second, that the sponsor is not demanding a huge marketing spend which might suit their own PR requirements but will eat into your revenues; and third, that the complete package for them – royalties, bulk buys at high discounts, revenue share, for example – leaves you with a reasonable profit to show from the exercise.

Costs, of course, do not just apply to production, although production does swallow the lion's share of investment resources. There are other things to consider. Will these books command higher than average royalties or advances? Will they require a big marketing spend? Consumer books publishers, for example, need to find significant sums of money to spend on high-profile books even before those books have got as far as the production department. A consumer books publisher who wants to make an impact with, let us say, a new line of cookery books has got a third party to deal with: literary agents. If agents are to encourage their clients to go to a house, they will need good evidence that the publisher is prepared to look after their authors in every respect. They will want a serious advance, they will want to see marketing and sales plans for their clients' books and they will certainly want to see those plans carried out.

As for advances, although it is now generally agreed that the way in which they spiralled a few years ago was quite damaging for the industry, there is no denying the fact that some classes of book do require significant advances because there are so many publishers competing to get them on their lists. Advances have now apparently dropped overall but it is still possible for them to zoom up in, for example, auctions where houses compete for titles. 'Showbiz' autobiographies or politicians' memoirs are favourite candidates for this kind of competition.

CASH FLOW

The issues raised above will have implications for cash flow. Cash flow dominates the minds of managing directors and financial directors, perhaps more so than profitability. Cash flow is about the amount of money in the company's bank account and the rate at which it moves in and out. It is particularly important at any point when a company decides to expand its output. Growth can be a dangerous phase for companies in any sector. The company finds itself investing in its product at an increased level, which means that it is going to have to find the money to pay for this. Unless the company has asked the shareholders, or the bank, effectively to give it a loan to cover these increased costs, it will find itself compromised financially, as costs will outweigh income until the point where the new product comes on stream and, we hope, sells at the rate projected.

Cash flow is not difficult to understand. Imagine your own bank account. Most of us proceed every month on the basis of ensuring that our expenditure does not exceed our income, and in the expectation that at the end of the month, money will flow in – our salaries. Our salaries are in normal circumstances guaranteed and they arrive at a precise time. However, in a publishing house, income can arrive at a variety of times, not all of which can be precisely predicted. Nor will it necessarily arrive when it is most needed. Income is dependent on customers buying our books. Can we depend on them absolutely to buy our books? We cannot, and that immediately brings uncertainty into the picture.

Risk is something that all publishers have to live with. The most successful ones are those who are best at judging risk. Even they, however, can be compromised by cash flow. Risk is about making judgements about the future. Cash flow is about the ability to pay the bills that are hitting the company now. So, as you put your new list into place, your finance director will be paying close attention to the level and rate of expenditure as those new books come on stream, and analysing whether the company's current frontlist and backlist sales are going to provide sufficient income to pay for your expansion. Remember, when we create new books, we have to pay the printing and other associated costs now. We may not see real income from those books perhaps for a year.

It is unlikely that you will be asked to work on cash flow projections, but your financial director is likely to be very concerned with the implications that flow from a new list, and therefore it is absolutely vital that you provide him or her with accurate forecasts on production costs, publication dates and sales figures.

RATE OF GROWTH AND INVESTMENT

You need to ask of a new list whether it is one where growth will be slow to begin with but, like good wine, 'If I lay it down now, will I be able to reap the rewards in about five years' time?' Education publishers put massive investment into books for the school curriculum but know that if they get those books right, the financial rewards can be enormous. Any publisher making this kind of investment is not going to get their money back fast, but the pay-off in the long run may be more than worthwhile.

Conversely, when the opportunity arises, several publishing houses will compete heavily for a list which another has decided to sell off because it no longer lies in the heartland of its business. Such competition can push the price up but the successful buyer calculates that the investment will be justified as it will increase the house's market share, and increase it immediately.

PROBLEM AREAS IN LIST DEVELOPMENT

MISJUDGING MARKET SIZE

Growth is a tricky area. Already mentioned are the hazards of entering a field too early or too late; or following a flash in the pan when you thought you were backing a trend. Even when a field does turn out to be relatively stable, you must consider whether the market has reached saturation point. Computer books are a good example. In the mid-1980s, publishers, observing that the pc market was expanding fast, entered the field with burgeoning lists. The number of books appearing in the shops suggested that the publishers assumed that every member of the population had bought a machine and would want to buy a book to go with it. There was a good market there, and a growing one, but not one big enough to sustain their publishing lists. They had not realised that most pc buyers would be perfectly content with the manual that came with their machines and would not feel the need to buy further publications. By confusing another manufacturer's growth with their own, many got their fingers burnt and dropped out, leaving the market to computer book publishers who understood the needs of the serious (usually professional) computer user.

ATTACKING THE COMPETITION HEAD-ON

It is always possible, even in publishing, for David to slay Goliath but note that David managed it in ways that Goliath was not expecting. Only the truly big and rich companies can afford to stand toe to toe and slug it out and many will eventually ruminate later on just how expensive it proved to be. If your company is prepared to back you in some all-out onslaught on a particular field, do your homework thoroughly beforehand, be completely convinced about your plans and, here is the rub, be prepared with the information, interpretation, analysis and calming influence that will be constantly required of you as expenditure increases.

It is in the nature of large corporations that they relish this kind of grandiose scheme. To be perfectly fair to them, when a corporation reaches a certain size, this is the rational way for them to behave. If you are big, act big. A medium-sized or small company simply cannot afford it and if you are an editor in such a company, you will be infinitely better off spotting a gap and developing that. This strategy may not have much glamour going for it but you will probably be providing sounder business for your house.

SERIES AS GROWTH CREATORS

A series is a wonderfully quick way of generating a lot of titles. An outside series editor is engaged, who is paid appropriately, to drum up interest and contract books working in conjunction with you. Series always start with the best intentions in the world. You and the series editor are keen, he or she has very good connections and can probably bring in good writers. You define the series and what you want to do with it and what you expect of it. Unhappily, however, after a year or so, during which everyone is as keen as mustard and the series editor is anxious to prove that the job is being done well, the rot inevitably sets in. A slightly less vigilant approach emerges, especially if the first few books in the series are successful. The series editor thinks that the task has been licked, the in-house editor feels that the series is working and relaxes. Sooner or later second-rate books arrive and are accepted. The need to keep pushing through titles in order to keep the momentum up leads to the inclusion of some that are not within the defined focus of the series.

Worse, the in-house editor begins to suspect that the series editor is assuming the power of patronage and is signing up books for all the wrong reasons. That editor may also wake up to the realisation that it is he or she who is actually providing the drive behind the commissioning of books for the series, while the series editor is taking all the glory and being paid for doing very little.

Series are not bad things in themselves. They do have the advantage of allowing you to gain a position quite quickly in a field. Really successful series can dominate the market in some areas. They can also be a strong indicator of your commitment to a subject area. However, keep yourself at centre stage and with a strong hand on the series editor's shoulder, otherwise you are virtually handing over the commissioning of the list to an outside party.

GUIDELINES FOR PAYING SERIES EDITORS

Series editors and advisers have to be paid appropriately. A series editor is an 'editor at large', working on behalf of you and your publishing house, although some working for educational or academic publishing are doing it mainly for career or prestige reasons. There are various options open.

You will probably have to consider some sort of retainer, which can be paid in one of two ways:

1 an annual flat fee; or
2 a fee to be paid when titles are signed up.

The first option does not necessarily encourage the series editor to go looking for books for the series, but it may be necessary to keep and attract an important person and it does mean that he or she may not be retained by another publisher to perform a similar task.

The second option does encourage them to bring in books and should be your desired option because effectively it means payment by results. The size of the fee will depend on the financial profile of the books being signed up, but should not be higher than the equivalent of 1 per cent of the total royalty earnings for the books on their first print run.

When paying an annual retainer, the fee should be the equivalent of the total fees the series editor might have earned on signing up books during the course of the year under option 2.

For both options it may be necessary to consider paying royalties to the series editor on every book published under his or her auspices, and many will ask for and expect to get a royalty. A royalty of 1 per cent should be acceptable.

Under both options you are giving the series editor the equivalent of 2 per cent royalty on every book published in the series. To this, don't forget, is added the author's royalty. Although each book is likely to be less profitable than if signed up by yourself (because each is bearing a higher than normal royalty charge), the series editor is in effect being paid the equivalent of part of an editor's salary, but that then allows you to publish more books and without incurring the extra overheads that come with employing an in-house editor.

There are two other important points to make:

- Agree with the series editor the number of titles he or she is expected to sign up under the series contract, especially when calculating an annual fee.
- Be prepared to pay for a minimum amount of expenses. You must resist notions about 'time spent' because you are likely to be faced with an open-ended bill, but you should certainly be prepared to reimburse stationery, postage, telephone and fax expenses, but only on sight of evidence of these expenses. It is best also to convey to the series editor the message that you are expecting any expenses of this sort to be used economically.

PLAYING COPY-CAT

There are editors who watch other publishers' lists and then use them as a crib to create ones of their own, quickly. The copy-cat editor may think that by imitating a list, he or she is replicating success and is able to avoid all the effort, cost, research and planning that went into the original article.

By copying new books which are currently being published, that editor is imitating work which was probably put in place several years ago. When his or her new books do come to publication, they stand a good chance of being out of date or out of fashion. In the process the editor will have skipped the proper disciplines of list building and done himself or herself no favours in terms of professional development.

CONCLUSION

Starting a new list can be a very exciting time in an editor's career development. The processes one goes through are mostly those that apply to individual book commissioning. What is different is the scale, and its implications for the resources of the house. One can compare it to starting a new, small business unit within the company. The experience of doing that can provide a real step up for the editor – a broader understanding of how the business works, and consequently, an increase in confidence and ability.

Lists are living things. The next chapter will turn to how one keeps them in good shape.

CASE STUDY

A thoroughly well-established and distinguished professional publisher had a series of print products focused on the public sector market which were highly successful. It had been estimated that their market penetration was something in the order of 75 per cent.

In view of the fact that the public sector was moving rapidly into digital functioning, the publishers decide to diversify their print product. They would keep the paper product but also now make it available on a CD Rom. In view of the great success of the print product, the publisher only took a few soundings along the lines of, 'If we made it also available on CD Rom, would you be interested in purchasing it?' Their questions met with approval. The publishers decided to produce a CD Rom to begin with and then put the material up on line. They were a bit concerned about putting it straight up on line because it is known that public sector networks are always crashing!

The CD was an exact replica of what was in the printed product, nothing more, nothing less. This was based on the assumption that there was additional value in the functionality and that the whole work would replace the print version. The price was higher. The CD Rom was roughly 20 per cent more expensive than the printed version. Sales of the CD were a huge disappointment, although print sales kept their level. What had gone wrong?

The publishers decided to commission some proper market research. They talked to customers who had bought the CD Rom and those who had not. They discovered that:

1 The publication was still highly appreciated as a print product but the respondents said that it had now been superseded by on-line requirements.
2 The market had not expected just a straightforward CD Rom version of the print product. They assumed that it would be different; that it would complement the print product by offering something different.
3 Customers kept the print product alongside the CD Rom version, so the price model was also wrong.
4 They indicated what they would like to see on the CD Rom, and on an on-line version. These suggestions mostly came under the heading of 'added value' – bulletins, diaries, conferences and archive.
5 They gave suggestions as to what they would find 'user friendly'.
6 The respondents had quite a lot to say about the products on offer from their competitors. What they said produced very useful information about content, structure, usage and pricing, all of which the publishers absorbed carefully.

As a result, after a lot of re-working, revenues increased by nearly three times and the publication is now up on line. There was increased investment in demonstrations, training and other support systems. The CD version is still preserved because of the anxieties about public sector digital networks, referred to earlier.

The publishers are very cautious about putting the prices of the on-line product up because they want to encourage migration to it. They constantly work on ways of making it even more user friendly. They have a data 'warehouse' which allows them to update content on a daily basis. Finally, they can conclude that the product is working.

QUESTION

This is simply a very good example of a publishing firm disobeying every rule about researching one's market when generating a new product. The publishers also blithely thought that the print product in another (but content-identical) form would, self-evidently, be something the market wanted and would pay a lot more for. How do you think they got themselves in this pickle? The constructive way in which they reacted afterwards shows that they knew how to go about solving the problem they had made for themselves.

Developing and maintaining a list

7

In this chapter we will look at:

- developing an established list
- developing a list as a competitive tool
- the backlist
- reprinting
- neglecting the backlist
- putting books out of print

Developing a list is not simply a continuous process of amassing hundreds of titles under some broad, generic heading and then saying, 'There, now we have a cookery/fiction/history/biology list.' All it proves is that the publisher does indeed have a lot of books but taken together the list shows very little discrimination, sense of purpose or focus.

Developing a list is a much more considered process. The editor is looking for a series of books that are strongly defined in the mind's eye in both editorial and marketing terms. The readers are targeted, so is the format in which they like to receive their books, the prices they are prepared to pay, the way in which they use their books, whether they buy their books through shops or by direct mail.

Publishing is a rather retrospective process. It is standard practice continually to look over our shoulders at what was done before, to see if it worked, and to judge books that are offered through that prism. This may not sound very adventurous – rarely is it possible to make a complete leap off into the dark – but it produces a reasonable enough judgement to allow us to proceed. The commercial risk will always be there – so much depends on how intelligently we construe the evidence we have from the recent past.

If the process of list development is to produce a 'family' of books, the apotheosis of list development is the creation of a backlist. Some consumer books publishers have them; all specialist publishers do.

So how in practical terms do you set about doing all this? Let us begin with the situation of inheriting a list already in print.

DEVELOPING AN ESTABLISHED LIST

For the vast majority of editors, their work will be focused on developing an existing list: refining, improving and growing it.

In order to plan to develop the list, you need to know what you are working with.

- How many titles per year has the current list been producing? Is it too few really to establish a strong presence, or has overproduction spread the quality too thinly?
- Does the level at which the titles are pitched actually match the targeted readership? Is the list producing monographs and supplementary texts, believing that students buy them? Or are your DIY manuals too technical for the needs of the amateur?
- What are the sales like? You are bound to find a range from excellent to dismal. Try to analyse the characteristics of those books which may have influenced sales performance. Rather than examine every book on the list, pick out examples of notably good, mediocre and abysmal sales, then go looking for clues. Look in the book files. What does the correspondence between the author and the editor, or the adviser and the editor, reveal? It could show a well-honed understanding on everyone's part of what the book was designed to do, or it could reveal that there were doubts or misgivings along the way – from which you can learn.
- Read the reviews in the promotion files. These will provide evidence from the first stage of critical approval. If your house has an inspection copy service, there are likely to be comments forms available, containing valuable opinions from the very people intended to read and recommend a text.
- Ask the sales manager if he or she recalls sales reports from reps that might shed some light on the sales performances.
- Talk to the college reps, if you have them, to obtain feedback on the reaction at grass-roots level.
- If your house is a heavy user of direct marketing, find out what proportion of the sales comes direct from the customer and what is sold through the bookshops. If the proportions are not what you expect, then there are questions to be asked about the emphasis of the marketing effort.

- Find out what proportion of sales come from the home market and what from export. There might be some unexpected surprises.
- Go travelling to the bookshops, universities, colleges, schools and conferences, depending on your sector of publishing. Ask people to give you their honest opinion of the list. How do you know to whom to talk? There are connections just waiting to be used: booksellers, authors, advisers, contributors, agents. Make appointments to see them (including bookshop managers) but ask your contact if he or she would be good enough to introduce you to other colleagues.
- Talk to colleagues in sales and marketing and ask for their impressions of the list. Many will have well-formed opinions of the publishing list and will be happy to have the opportunity to discuss it candidly. Requesting an opportunity to talk properly with your colleagues does give everyone the chance to focus on the subject in a way that is quite different from ad hoc conversations.

By now much valuable information will have been gathered. This must be worked through assiduously and systematically, to produce an analysis of what is good or bad about the list, or a mixture of both.

You will now have a strengths-and-weaknesses analysis on which to build. This will offer distinct pointers to what you, as the new editor, must continue doing in order to replicate past and current successes, or what to avoid if you are to steer clear of the failures. Although you will now know what you are working with, ideas will be needed in order to move on from there, to give you lift-off.

THE TYRANNY OF IDEAS

No book can teach you how to create ideas. A substantial element of that comes from an individual's intrinsic talents. There are people who are genuinely creative. They can think laterally; they can suddenly synthesise something focused and unique out of a seeming welter of fragmented thoughts or information; they are good at making connections; they have the ability intuitively to grasp at what interests people. Do not despair, for even if you are not one of these genuinely original types, you can generate ideas. But instead of pushing yourself, frightened by an inner voice that says 'I must have ideas, I must have ideas', learn to listen and absorb – first.

Ideas come from all directions, if only you know it, and ideas are about making connections between one thing and another. They seldom exist in isolation. Every day you can pick up information about what people are interested in or want from authors, advisers, booksellers, let alone television, radio, newspaper and magazines. That process of talking to 'opinion formers', which you went through earlier, is bound to generate ideas. Your job now is to match those sources of interest with a product that satisfies them, and at the appropriate level. Once you have generated your ideas, they must be tested against the opinions of fellow editors, publishing directors, marketing colleagues, authors, agents, advisers and known experts.

Authors will be needed, to match these ideas. They might be found on your backlist, or you may recognise them as established writers in a particular field, or they could be recommended to you.

The process is one of focusing down and down until you have what is needed – a book or product that, by all accounts, fits a particular need or interest and the author or authors who have the resources to write the content and the skills to pitch at the level the market wants. This is the essence of list building: developing a series of books that possess a coherence around that part of the market you are attacking. It must be emphasised that all of this must be done with reference to the marketing resources of your company. If you have defined your market and the product you want to supply, do you have the resources to reach it?

NICHE LIST BUILDING

In reality niche books are a rare commodity. Perhaps facsimile publishing of rare and ancient books or manuscripts would truly qualify for the label. *Niche* really means that some publisher somewhere has spotted a precise need for a particular sort of book, with a particular sort of reader who wants it in a particular sort of format with a corresponding price, and knows how to market it successfully to the point where the publisher dominates the field. Frankly, it is rather meaningless; we could say the same thing of any well-focused list. The principles which have guided a niche publisher can be followed by any editor, in any sort of publishing, who is prepared to approach list building with research, planning, analysis, follow-through and patience.

DEVELOPING A LIST AS A COMPETITIVE TOOL

A list can be used as a weapon in two respects: in relation to authors and to the competition.

AUTHORS

There is some evidence that many hopeful authors are publisher 'blind'. Already you have probably received too many publishing proposals from authors who seem to have very little idea of which publishers would be suitable for their books. There is a second class of authors who do have some sense of appropriate homes for their books but whose main preoccupation is simply to get published by one of them. The third class are authors who form quite definite views of publishing houses – they have likes and dislikes, and quite often they know a lot about the houses, their editors, and their marketing departments. They will choose which houses they want to publish their books. These authors are discriminating because they are often experienced and successful.

Authors (and their agents) approach publishers because they like their lists. They are attracted to them and want to become part of them. It is true that authors also seem to be attracted to editors and often follow them from one house to another. The editor is the one who creates and develops a list and therefore, to a degree, the list and the editor are synonymous.

The whole process of crafting, building, developing and focusing a list is a vital part of drawing authors to a publishing house. How can an author feel important or good about being in print with a publisher who seems to have no sense of discrimination in their list building? Authors want and need to feel good about themselves, and they want their peers to recognise they are working with a publisher of judgement and authority. Once a list does appear to the outside world to have been carefully put together, and carefully marketed, it does become a tremendous source of attraction to authors.

For an editor, reaching the point where one's list is where authors want to be, life has to get easier. You no longer have to fight for authors or gain their approval. In all likelihood, the authors are passing on your name to others. You may find that your rate of submissions increases – something of a mixed blessing – and that the hit rate for quality submissions also grows. You have now reached the point where you are 'established'.

KEEPING THE COMPETITION OUT

This same cohesion, planning and focusing similarly give the editor strength when competing against other publishers. Not only do the authors beat a path to the editor's door, but that same editor, by meticulous list building, is creating depth and strength in a particular field which a competitor will find hard to beat. Competitors will always attempt the occasional sally into someone else's area if they can see that publisher flourishing, but unless they are prepared to go into the proper depth and care of planned list building (which often takes years to come to fruition) they will not succeed.

THE BACKLIST

The content of a book will define whether it has backlist potential or not. The question to ask is, will the demand for this book continue at a steady pace over a matter of years, or is it a book that once read is soon forgotten. The author is a very important part of this too. It's unlikely that Ruth Rendell's publishers keep her books alive on their backlists because her readers keep wanting to replace their much thumbed paperback editions. Many people, once hooked by the first novel of hers they read, will then want to buy the others she has written. There is always a new generation of people coming along ready to be obsessed by detective stories and so the process simply repeats itself.

Specialist publishers seldom have star writers in this way although there have been some who have made a small fortune for their publishers. However, in just the same way, the demand for the book is content-driven: the content is so good, so well tailored to the needs of the reader that new generations of students, researchers, school children, practitioners, buy it year after year because it is just what they need to help them get on top of their subject.

Indeed, some specialist authors are very good self-promoters. They are happy to turn up to speak at conferences and push their books. In fact, more often than not, they come up with the idea of doing this. You will need to take a view on whether this proposed sales pitch is going to work or whether you are dealing with an author with an over-endowed sense of salesmanship that does not match the inside of the book. Particularly beware of authors who ask to be sent to overseas conferences, all expenses paid, because they are convinced this will lead to tremendous sales. It might, but it should be you who decides to push the boat out.

DEVELOPING A BACKLIST

Strictly speaking, a backlist cannot be developed. A backlist is a frontlist that translates into ongoing demand. If the new books you acquire do not have sticking power, there is nothing you or the marketing department can do to convince anyone that you are a backlist publisher.

It is most important to remember that although specialist publishers are almost inevitably backlist publishers, backlist potential is not subject-related.

Most new books make reasonable sales in the first year. The question to be asked is whether those sales can be replicated in the years following? Indeed, is it possible to increase sales in the second, third or even fourth year of a book's life? Some examples:

- An academic monograph should make the bulk of its sales in the first year, when most of the world's scholarly libraries buy it. Once they have bought it, the market for it is more or less exhausted. In sales terms it is effectively dead, even though perhaps for 10 years, people will take it off the shelves and consult it. While they are still doing that, however, the book is a good advertisement for your list!
- A novel from a gifted writer which is well reviewed will result in excellent sales in its first year and will probably reprint. But what will determine its ability to stay on the backlist thereafter is whether the writer becomes established. Ruth Rendell was mentioned earlier. There are lots of other examples: Terry Pratchett, Anne Tyler, Danielle Steel, Ian McKewan. Their books are displayed in the shops prominently. Once established in this way, they attract new readers year after year.
- An educational publisher can launch a new textbook and in the first two years of its life it may sell very slowly, in spite of good reviews. But the education system is such that teachers have comparatively little time to inspect new books; they have to compare them with texts they are currently using; they have to agree with colleagues that they will adopt a new text; their budgets for buying new books will determine when they can make purchases. Consequently, the period from publication to purchases coming on stream can be stretched out but once these sales begin to bite and the books become adopted for curriculum use, the publisher knows he or she can expect sustained and increasing sales for some years to come.

All the principles that are applied while developing a frontlist hold equally well here. In addition, however, you are purposefully looking for books that can be kept in print for at least several years. That means you are looking for staying power.

- The books have the potential for sustained use, with one set of buyers succeeding another in the following years. Typically these books would be publications designed for educational, academic and professional courses and training. Unless the courses change, or a competitor enters the field, successfully, the books will enjoy sales year on year.
- Equally, the books can be published for consumer markets where there is a strongly perceived and sustained general interest; for example, cookery, gardening and travel. Into this category also fall fiction writers with a following.
- These books have quality. They have been well researched, they focus accurately on their readership, the authors have high-order writing skills. The material is presented in a format and style that the readership finds user friendly, comfortable or stimulating. High-minded

interpretations of 'quality' have to be laid aside. A consistently successful writer of 'sex and shopping' novels may still be a quality writer.

Add to these characteristics the concept of coherence, which was covered in the sections on lists (pages 21–2). The intention is to build a 'family' of books that will stay in print and develop an effective 'presence' in that area. Although many consumer books are purchased as impulse buys, the habitual book buyer begins to discern what 'labels' to look for, confident that these are the kinds of books he or she likes to read. There is a recognition factor that can literally be translated into the design of the jacket and spine.

Books that can be reprinted are profitable books. They more than justify the effort put into picking them for their robust ability to stand the test of time. Furthermore, they need to be looked after by their editors so that they maintain their value. Tending the backlist can entail the following activities.

REPRINTING

Printing technology has changed so much in recent years that it is now possible to reprint any quantity you like, even one copy, and to do it quickly and cost-effectively. This flexibility should not blind you to the need to exercise judgement over reprinting, and the timing of reprints. If you want to make the best out of the profitability that reprinting brings, choose reprint quantities that will allow you to keep your unit costs cut to the bone. There are still disciplines to be followed:

- Avoid the cardinal sin of running out of stock. There is a well-known axiom in publishing that if a customer goes into a bookshop to buy a book and is told that it is out of stock but that a reprint will soon arrive, the customer never goes back. No one has ever scientifically tested that but there is enough anecdotal evidence to suggest that there is more than a nugget of truth in it.
- How do you choose your moment? Companies differ in their systems for stock control, but all computer-generated systems can immediately tell you how many copies have been sold and how many are left to sell. In addition, the computer can present the unsold stock situation in terms of how many months' or weeks' stock is left if the book carries on selling at its current level. You must allow for sufficient time to get a reprint done.
- You must 'police' your stock reports regularly. Too many editors put these on one side as a chore, to be attended to when other things are less pressing. Make it a task that you automatically attend to on at

least a monthly basis if you are a specialist publisher or on a weekly basis if you are, say, a consumer books publisher whose stock moves more quickly. In consumer houses, it is the sales and marketing department who are most likely to police stock levels.

- Let your author know you are reprinting and ask if there are any corrections to be made. There is a huge difference between genuine corrections and rewriting large chunks of a book. You must make it clear you are asking for corrections.
- You should examine the sales pattern carefully. Look for large stocks moving, say, to your North American distributor. Are they likely to come back? Perhaps you ought to check availability of stock in your other overseas distributors before reprinting. You might choose to bring some of that stock back.
- For a new consumer title, where the reps have done an exceptionally good job selling in, you perhaps ought to check with the marketing department that the book is actually moving out of the shops before doing an early reprint. There have been examples of celebrity autobiographies that failed with the reading public, even though the shops subscribed to those titles with enthusiasm.

REJACKETING REPRINTS

If a book has a distinctive jacket, however dated it looks, everyone recognises it and that has many advantages. There once was a social work text whose jacket made the editor cringe every time she saw it. Admittedly the cringing began some years after it was first published, when the jacket had begun to date. However, she was loath to change it because the book's sales were excellent, and consistently so year after year, and she knew that in the market-place it was known as the 'chessboard book' because a chessboard was featured in the design of the jacket. She felt anxious about removing that mark of instant recognition.

She might have taken a different view if a competitor had subsequently introduced a text that was going to challenge the prime position that her book held in the market-place. She might then have decided that her book needed to be dressed in some smart new clothes, to renew interest in it and convince buyers that it was still up to the challenge of the competitor's new text.

In consumer publishing it is now regarded as best practice to change the livery of the most successful parts of the backlist on a regular basis as there is evidence that this does lead to increased sales. In all probability it is an effective way of introducing younger readers to backlist books that may have been in print for a number of years. A contemporary jacket is more likely to catch their eye. For the retail sector there is a strong implicit message in rejacketing: we believe in the quality of our backlist so strongly that we are prepared to bear the cost of creating brand-new jackets.

ADJUSTING PRICES

The cost of reprinting books is always lower than the cost of producing the book from scratch because offsetting costs are much lower than the cost of origination. It is perfectly possible, therefore, for backlist prices to remain quite stable year after year, while the prices of new books continually rise. Backlist publishing is profitable publishing. Costs are relatively contained and sales are reasonably predictable and assured. While so many resources are by necessity pumped into the creation and marketing of new books, here is one area where a publisher can achieve good profits. Not only are the production costs lower, but so are promotion and marketing costs. The book is already known in the market-place and the necessity of pushing and publicising it diminishes, although repromoting the backlist can often be a very worthwhile exercise in terms of sales.

All the more reason therefore to maximise the profits to be made on these books, and that means maintaining prices at the same levels as your new titles. However tempting it is to keep last year's titles at last year's prices because the cost of reprinting is low, resist the temptation. Remember that those extra profits on the backlist will help with the investment of perhaps more speculative new books.

If you work in consumer publishing, the likelihood is that your colleagues in sales and marketing will have made the pricing adjustment for you. In specialist publishing, marketing will also have a strong say on pricing. In one house, the marketing director suggested that instead of pricing all books at, say, £10.95 or £12.95, all prices should be rounded up to one penny short of a pound – i.e. £10.99 or £12.99. He calculated that this would bring in an extra £200,000 of revenue, essentially without anyone having to lift a finger. Everyone agreed with his suggestion.

NEW EDITIONS

When your much cherished backlist title shows signs of ageing, or signs of being attacked by new competition, it is time to consider if a new edition is required. Not all books can go into new editions, possibly because of some quirk in the content, and not all authors want to provide a new edition. All other things being equal, however, a new edition is advisable if it will allow your book to maintain its position in the market-place.

- A new edition should be an attacking rather than a defensive move. If a bold newcomer has entered the market, it is a bit late in the day to start organising a new edition when the competition is already in print and stealing sales from you. Most good editors know what the 'staple items' in their backlist are and evaluation of the need for a new edition and its timing should be a regular process undertaken in conjunction with the authors.
- The publication of a new edition should also be taken in conjunction with the stock levels of the old edition. Ideally, the new edition should come on stream just as the stock of the old edition is finally draining away. Here is another instance where you must emphasise the importance of getting the author to deliver on time. If the author does not, you will be forced either to live with an awkward gap while demand still continues, or to do a very small, therefore unprofitable, reprint of the old edition just to fill that gap.
- Remember that these days we live in the 'information age'. Information comes at us constantly and gets updated frequently. If a book is successful, it is more likely to go into new editions sooner and more often than it would have in the past.

NEGLECTING THE BACKLIST

If you are following the principles referred to above – reprinting on time, in the right quantity, rejacketing when necessary, keeping your prices current – then you might ask how can you neglect it? Possibly, but there is more to tending the backlist than good housekeeping. One keeps a home clean but may not necessarily be interested in it. Cleaning is merely a way of avoiding mess and dirt. Similarly you can keep the backlist materially in good shape simply because it stops stock control and marketing nagging at you about reprints. The backlist is a living thing, even if it does not confront you in the immediate way that the frontlist does.

A proactive view of the backlist as something that you observe and analyse as an overall part of your editorial strategy is an infinitely better approach than the one of simply ensuring that books stay in stock.

You are dependent on maintaining the sales of these books. No publisher is prepared to use more than minimal marketing resources on backlist books; marketing spend is reserved for the frontlist. You can have some impact on the marketing machine, however, at relatively little cost.

- Examine the catalogue. How are the backlist books laid out? Are they being presented effectively? Is good use being made of quotes from reviews?

- If your marketing department is planning a campaign for a new title, do you have backlist titles that could 'piggyback' on that campaign?
- Are you ensuring that the most appropriate backlist titles are being sent for display at conferences and exhibitions?
- Is it about time that you persuaded the marketing department that they should mount a backlist campaign, not across the board but a focused one that promotes you as the leading publisher in your field?

Although many publishers' backlist titles do appear to sell themselves, these are titles that are gradually ageing and therefore inevitably in danger of being swept aside by the thrill of the new. They therefore need your care and attention, especially if you are looking after a backlist that someone else originated. Psychologically it is often more difficult to nurture another editor's list, but you must.

PUTTING BOOKS OUT OF PRINT

Probably too many books go out of print without our noticing or caring. It is difficult to maintain passion for so many books, backlist and frontlist. However, editors most commonly are given responsibility for deciding whether or not a book should remain in print. We may not notice the precise moment when the book goes out of stock, but the decision to kill it off remains ours. That decision is made in conjunction with assessing future stock needs.

First, stock control informs the editor that stocks are running low; often a stock reorder level has been previously set. At that point the editor decides whether a reprint should be produced or not. If it is the latter, because sales are too low, then stock control is instructed to flag the book in the system as going out of print at nil stock.

Secondly, if a book, unhappily, is selling very badly indeed, then a tough decision must simply be made to take the book off the lists and to remainder or pulp the remaining stock. It is arguably more expensive to keep a very slow-selling book in print, with the ongoing costs of warehousing and other overheads, than to get rid of it. Most publishing houses hold a stock valuation exercise of this sort once or twice a year to ensure that 'dead wood' is cleared out of the warehouse. In all likelihood, the editor will be consulted about this. If so, the following should be borne in mind:

- It is wasteful and pointless to fight to keep books in print that are simply not earning their keep. Many editors resist pulping or remaindering books for quite emotional reasons – they simply do not want to let go of them.

- Sometimes you do have to point out that there are titles that must remain in print for good 'political' or marketing reasons. It is pointless remaindering *Cymbeline* however badly it sells in relation to the rest of your Shakespeare texts if you claim to have a complete edition of Shakespeare in print. Similarly with the complete works of Freud or Jung. Or, for example, you might have a distinguished author whom another publisher is trying to poach from you. Right now would be the very worst moment to put one of his or her beloved texts out of print. In that kind of situation, prune back overstocks severely, but leave enough in the warehouse to allow the book to go selling on quietly.
- If you do have to put a book out of print, always remember to inform the author with a polite but firm letter explaining why you have had to take the decision. Otherwise, the first the author is likely to hear of it is when a royalty statement comes. This is discourteous and the author is likely to be upset. Furthermore, the author might want to take the opportunity to purchase a few more copies of the book before it becomes unobtainable.

Some time in the future, there will be no such things as out-of-print books. All books will have been captured digitally and will therefore be easily accessible for production purposes. Combined with printing on demand, this should mean you can always fulfil sales. However, there are very many books in print that have not been captured digitally and until they are, they are not subject to this kind of flexibility. Some of the larger houses are already beginning to digitise their entire catalogue of books so that they will never be out of print.

CASE STUDIES

1 A schools book publisher, operating in a highly competitive market, decided to develop the list's core-curriculum publishing – mathematics – by diversifying into the lower end of the ability range. Market research – done by academics – had shown that in terms of helping these children, there had to be a need for publications that focused on them.

The series was launched and sales were very disappointing. The publishers decided to find out why and talked to their market. They discovered that the cash-hungry schools felt they could not afford to buy books devoted to just one part of their school intake. In order to make their money go further, they preferred series that were aimed at the entire ability continuum.

On discovering this, the publishers nevertheless resisted adding mixed ability books to the series. They were convinced the series would work. Eventually, they changed their mind, especially when one of the main competitors launched a new mixed ability series. The publisher's series by now suited nobody. The competitor's success caused their own modest sales to plummet. Two new books were already in the pipeline and £50,000 had already been invested in both. Nevertheless, the publishers pulled the plug on those two books and exited before any more blood was spilled.

QUESTION

Why do you think the publishers did not check on the application of academic research to the needs of schools? Why did they not know how the sensibilities of schools work when it comes to spending money? Why did they persist in the face of early failure?

2 A professional publisher working in the area of psychodynamics had a fairly elderly book about bereavement on her list. It was aimed for professionals working with the bereaved, but was also accessible to the intelligent lay reader. The sales, which in the beginning had been good, had now dropped dramatically and she was under constant pressure to put it out of print. She persisted with it because at the time, there were very few books on the subject in print.

To her astonishment, one day an order came through from her Australian subsidiary, requesting 9,000 copies. She double checked as to whether a couple of zeros had been added to the number by mistake. They had not. The author had been on a highly successful nation-wide tour and customers were clamouring for copies. She looked at her stock and found she had 2,500 copies in the warehouse. Actually, she knew she had 2,500 copies in the warehouse because the same colleagues who were urging her to put the book out of print, were also urging her to pulp that stock. The fact is that she had too much stock because she had last reprinted at a time when sales were quite good, and assumed they would continue on that way.

She shipped out almost all the stock, and decided to take the risk and reprint the rest of the Australian order. She felt it was a risk because if the Australians had misjudged demand, they would have a perfect right to ship back all that unsold stock. She also printed a few more for herself, just in case it came in handy back home.

All copies were sold in both countries. News of the growing influence of this author's work seemed to be generating new demand at home too. The publisher suspected that it had found in practice, not just in theory, an additional market – the intelligent lay reader existed! For the next reprint she decided to rejacket the book and throw some more money behind a promotion campaign. The book carried on like a rocket. It is now a classic used by counsellors and therapists, and read by ordinary people who may have to grapple with the effects of bereavement.

QUESTION

Do you think it is fair that the publisher should have benefited from her early mistake in reprinting far too many copies of the book? Do you now believe in luck as one of the most important elements of success in publishing? Do you have any books on your list which you suspect may be dying but might rise like Lazarus? Will you have the nerve to resuscitate them and how would you persuade your colleagues?

Teamwork and professional ethics 8

In this chapter we will look at:

- positive and negative aspects of teamwork
- getting the best out of your authors
- getting the best out of yourself
- bad behaviour

In connection with every aspect of an editor's activity, constant reference has been made to colleagues in other departments of the publishing house and the ways in which everyone works, or should work, together. This is no accident because now it is broadly recognised that an editor is only one person within a team of many, all of whom combine to publish a book successfully.

Not so long ago editors were seen as gifted individuals all doing their own thing. Teamwork, if it was visible, was somehow the natural outcome of a socially gregarious group of people working alongside each other.

In this chapter we look at the importance of consciously applying yourself to good teamwork, not taking it for granted, and not perceiving it as something to do with serendipity. Whatever individual talents, strengths, flair the editor brings to the process, if they are embellished by the combined efforts of a team of people working together for the benefit of the book, the difference is palpable and the greater the chance of success.

The team includes not only colleagues in the publishing house. It also includes your authors.

IN-HOUSE TEAMWORK

INFORMING

Editors should not need to be told about the importance of communication since they work in the communication business. Books may speak for themselves, and so should editors. It is tempting to say that you can never inform your colleagues enough – most things are relevant. But colleagues can suffer from information overload and it is important to judge what their information needs are before attempting to fulfil them. If in doubt, however, at least be guilty of giving them rather too much than too little. At the very least, you will not be judged as not knowing anything about your books.

- Give information on time.
- Give information tailored to the needs of the particular groups of colleagues you are working with.
- Give information as the system of your house requires it. The system has been set up to ensure that books are published efficiently throughout all your markets. If you do not think that the system is very good, try to persuade senior colleagues about ways in which it could be improved. If you do not like it, do not subvert it constantly because it will throw others off balance and they will not necessarily thank you for that. It is far more effective to persuade colleagues, if you have the conviction, evidence and ideas, that it could be bettered. You will be given credit for eventual improvements.
- Always keep hard copies of important emails between yourself and your authors on file. If you are off sick, on holiday – or maybe you've even left the job – there must be a record of important discussions that took place for your colleagues to access.

EXPLAINING

Remember that not everyone in the house knows the book from the inside out the way you do. You have been working closely on the book, in one way or other, for some time. What is immediately apparent to you, may not be to others. If you want others to be as familiar with it as you are, you must be prepared to explain many aspects of it, and in detail. This requires some patience, especially if you have to do it several times. Colleagues will appreciate your taking the time and making the effort, and are likely to develop positive feelings about you and your books.

ENTHUSIASM

Enthusiasm is catching. The sight and sound of an editor madly keen and intent on telling the world about the virtues of a particular book and why it is going to sell is galvanising to others around. Remember, however, that there is a difference between conviction and hype and that the difference shows. Remember, too, that no one wants to hear an editor going on and on and on – especially at a sales conference – about that book. A little, well-placed and well-thought-through conviction will go a long way. Only practice will lead to the best selling pitch. Watch others carefully as you talk about the book. When people start to look bored and restless, you have lost them. Do not try to rescue yourself by trying another tack. Learn to know when to stop.

The key to your enthusiasm is how you feel about the book. If you have not properly understood it, or who will read it and why anyone should buy it, you will fail to convince anyone else.

Remember that the process of generating enthusiasm begins the moment the idea for the book has hit the house because from that moment on, you have to involve everyone who will work on it. It is particularly important to get marketing on side. So, for example, if you are going to meet an author who is either going to provide a guaranteed winner, or even poses a slight risk, take one of your marketing colleagues along with you.

FORGIVENESS

Publishing is high-pressure and sometimes stressful work. At worst, there will be times in your career when you will want the forgiveness and understanding of others for books you commissioned that did not quite work out as well as hoped. At best, you will require others' toler ance for those silly little mistakes made when typescripts are flying all around and authors are chasing you. The process is reciprocal. Others are under pressure too and will similarly want your understanding.

There is a fine line to be drawn between understanding and indulgence. Any colleague who repeatedly makes mistakes is clearly a problem. The best way to deal with it is to refer the problem to someone more senior since there is a competence issue here. Losing your temper is never a good thing, although it might temporarily bring you a sense of relief, because it is likely to compound the problem.

UNDERSTANDING OTHERS' DIFFICULTIES

An important part of teamwork is a good basic understanding of your colleagues' work and the particular difficulties they face. If you have that, at the very least, you are not so likely to ask for the impossible from them. A surprising number of editors find it difficult to make the effort to develop a good understanding of production processes or marketing and can land themselves in tricky situations out of sheer ignorance, promising things to the author that they cannot guarantee.

A bonus that derives from developing a good understanding of your colleagues' work is that if anyone tries to mislead you, they are not likely to succeed.

INVOLVEMENT

Involvement is a constant process which does not stop when a particular job has come to an end. Remember to tell the colleagues who helped you with a successful book just how the sales or reviews are going. Talk to them about similar projects that are coming up. Ask their advice and hope they ask for yours. As an editor, it is easy to think that only *you* are really interested in the publishing programme, that only *you* care about the ways in which the lists are developing. But equally so can colleagues in sub-editorial, production and marketing. Indeed, talking to them about the way in which your editorial work is generally going helps them to develop their thinking about how their own contribution, or skills, can be improved.

AVOIDING ELITISM

Elitism would undeniably have been implicit in the understanding of an editor's role not so many years ago. Editors were the elite, especially in their own eyes. The editorial function was primordinate; other functions were seen as 'servicing'. Marketing took second place in an era when content ruled and when decisions about how to sell a book emerged only as a consequence of the decision to publish it. That is, sign up the book and we will decide later if and how we can sell it, and at what price. Production was seen as a tool of editorial, often following the editor's ideas about design.

Much of that has now changed as the power base in publishing has shifted, certainly towards marketing at a time when the ability to market goods effectively is seen as the hallmark of a successful company; and to an extent, in the direction of production. All publishing houses are now very cost-conscious. Production has a huge part to play in the control of costs. Many companies have developed standardised systems for design and production giving production departments control over an important part of the whole process. Production departments also have a major role to play in the digitisation of products. Furthermore, the importance of visual impact, in all sorts of publishing – including specialist publishing – has moved production departments progressively away from places that just dealt with the setting of words.

Whatever changes in the scenery have taken place, editorial elitism is far less pronounced than it used to be. It is very difficult to motivate others around you when they are made to feel unimportant; arrogance is never attractive and more often than not is entirely misplaced. Editors need their colleagues to be on their side, for the sake of their books.

AVOIDING DEPARTMENTALISM

Nothing is more dangerous to successful teamwork than departmentalism. This does not refer to justifiable pride in your particular sphere, but more to a fierce identification with your part in the process which can lead to rigid lines of division and responsibility and which from time to time breaks out into open antagonism and aggression. Mutual suspicion is rife and manifests itself in a lack of confidence in other departments to do their jobs properly. With everyone blaming everyone else, no one wants to take responsibility. People who work in publishing houses that function along these lines are working under stress, and can get addicted to working aggressively. However, it is the books that suffer the most.

WORKING WITH AUTHORS

Various broad principles are outlined here, many of which are mirrored in what has just been said about working with colleagues.

NURTURING VERSUS INDULGENCE

You find out the hard way about indulging when you discover that there seems no end to the demands an author wants to make. Authors have a job to do and we must expect a degree of professionalism from them too, because they certainly will expect it from us. Mutual respect is built on an understanding that both parties will do their professional best and that neither will take liberties. It is therefore important that respect is earned so that the editor has real authority. Authority will certainly be undermined if the author comes to believe that he or she can have agreement to almost everything. There are many aspects of book publishing which an author knows nothing or very little about, however much peripheral knowledge he or she has picked up along the way. It is the editor's job to pull the author up short at any point where that author is beginning to intervene or make demands that are neither practical nor likely to have a positive effect on the book.

KEEPING AUTHORS INFORMED

A happy author is often an author who has been given a good basic grounding in what is happening to his or her book. It can involve giving the author a detailed explanation of the processes that a book goes through and when; explaining your work and how you make decisions. This is a useful exercise because to many authors (especially first-time authors) the publishing house and the publishing process is a complete mystery and for many, the very fact that they have no real grasp of the situation can generate additional anxiety. They feel powerless and will react to that by trying to exert their own sense of power, often in a hostile way.

It also includes, of course, passing on information promptly and clearly, answering emails and letters in a timely fashion, and returning telephone calls. The number of editors who 'deal with' authors basically by ignoring them and not getting in touch except when they choose to is legion. Imagine being on the receiving end of that and how you would feel.

MAKING THE RELATIONSHIP RECIPROCAL

Here each side knows and understands its rights and obligations. Quite frequently, in real life, one side dominates the other and information and demands flow in one direction only. An editor or an author who thinks that he or she is the only one who matters or who calls the shots is bound to hit trouble sooner or later.

There are many stories about well-known consumer books authors who have become infamous for their demands, their tantrums and their spectacular losses of temper. It is probably impossible ever to work with these people in a genuinely reciprocal way. They have a good sense of their commercial appeal, believe that no one in the house will ever contradict them for fear of losing them to another publisher, and are probably driven themselves by large amounts of anxiety and ego. Fortunately for them, there are usually other publishers prepared to take on their next books because they have not fully anticipated how these authors are going to behave.

We all take stories about bad behaviour with a pinch of salt, but be wary of authors who have moved around a lot.

When an editor treats the publication process as an entirely one-sided affair, the author gets excluded from decisions and is made to feel as though publishing his or her book is a big favour. There is something entirely illogical about this. On the one hand the author is considered good enough to have written a book that you have chosen to publish.

On the other hand, that author is thought too stupid or ignorant to have anything relevant to contribute to the publication of the book.

KNOWING WHEN AND HOW TO SAY 'NO'

Experience tells you when it is time to draw a halt to something simply because you have been there before. If you have not learnt enough about production processes, or how marketing really works, so that you can refuse an author something that is simply not feasible or too costly, then clearly you still have some way to go on the learning curve. Everyone has been in that position at some point in their careers. When in doubt, always say that you need to check something out with your colleagues in other departments and will get back to the author. At least you will be on firmer ground when you have to refuse a demand because by now you will know something about it.

When you know that the answer should be 'no', there are two options available. Either you refuse, politely, but give full reasons; or, under pressure, you give in, knowing that capitulation is going to lead to further difficulties. Eventually somebody (if not you) is going to have to disappoint that author, who will conclude that either you do not know your job or have no power within the house. In which case, you have made yourself look foolish.

Saying 'no' entails choosing your moment, being courteous (especially when you know your refusal is going to cause disappointment) and backing your decision with a careful and thoroughly informed explanation as to how and why it has to be that way.

BAD BEHAVIOUR

EDITORS AS 'STARS'

It is better that others think you are a 'star' than that you think it yourself. If you do, you are in danger of becoming more famous for your celebrity status than for the excellent books you publish, and in the long run, vanity will lead to over-confidence. There are stars in the industry but they have been tried and tested over many years and have not lost their touch. They have earned their status.

GOING IT ALONE

It is always bad policy to work in isolation from your colleagues. It is equally bad policy to claim that a book's success is all yours. If you have managed to do all the sub-editing, production and marketing then either you work in a one-person outfit or you are a miracle worker. The first situation is more likely than the second.

PASSING THE BLAME AROUND

When something goes wrong, the chances are that at least some of the responsibility for the problem lies with you. There is no reason to take the blame for other people's incompetence but it is always worth asking yourself if you have contributed to it in some way. It is seldom 'all the fault of marketing/production/sales'.

NEGLECT

Unfortunately, the moment that something appears to be sewn up, whether it is a book, a whole programme, or a list, and that you can just ignore it for while, the situation somehow contrives to move out of control. The gardening principle is a good one to follow. Always move around, inspecting, seeing what needs tending or digging up or replanting.

FAVOURITISM

We all have favourites amongst colleagues and authors; this is a perfectly human behaviour. However, when you are habitually turning down colleagues' and authors' plans, ideas and requests, it is worth considering whether your personal dislike is colouring your judgement. For example, editors have been heard, during candid moments, to be quite censorious and punitive about certain authors and colleagues and to enjoy being in the position of denying them things that they want. This is a luxury you must do without in order to make the best of your publishing. Furthermore, when your colleagues hear you being scathing about someone else, they are bound to ask, 'I wonder what she says about me' or 'I'd better watch what I say to him'.

REALLY BAD BEHAVIOUR

Arrogance, egocentrism and bombast are essential elements in every editor's armoury. A touch of all three is an entirely necessary spur which drives editors forward and gives them the guts to choose what gets published and to push and shout for the books at every opportunity. When it gets out of hand, and especially when it appears to be self-serving, it is thoroughly unattractive and quite counter-productive. Only the most exceptionally gifted editors can get away with being prima donnas.

COMPETING WITH YOUR AUTHORS

It is bad manners and bad psychology to try to compete intellectually and creatively with authors. The bottom line is that if you, the editor, know so much and are so clever, why don't you write the books too. The author has taken the risk and made the effort to write the book. Allow the author a special place and respect.

CASE STUDY

An editor who was new to the job asked for a meeting with an author on the forward list, contracted to deliver her typescript fairly soon. The book was regarded as a potentially strong one, which is why the editor requested the meeting, so that he could get a progress report and establish a good working relationship with her. At the meeting, the author announced that not only was she going to be about six months late but that the book would be roughly 20 per cent over length, and she was including 25 illustrations. She said that the editor's predecessor had agreed this verbally with her. As the editor had looked through the file before the author arrived, he knew there was no mention of any of this. He therefore expressed some surprise but said he would look into this. The meeting ended, therefore, somewhat up in the air but the editor was left with a strong impression that the author was someone who expected to have her own way.

Not long after, at a publishing 'do', the editor was talking to a colleague in another publishing house, and discovered that his author was also writing a book for that house, with a delivery date just before the delivery date contracted for his house. Although the book was in the same subject area, it was not in competition with his, therefore this was not a contractual case of conflict of interest.

The editor came to the sad and quick realisation that the situation was infinitely more complicated than the one he had already thought he was in. Not only did he have a book that was going to be later, much longer, and also, because of the illustrations, much more expensive to produce, but his book was competing for the author's time.

QUESTIONS

If you were in this position, how do you think you would go about:

- dealing with the question of the promises given by your predecessor?
- getting the author to deliver a book closer in parameters to the one contracted?
- tackling the question of late delivery?
- accommodating to the other book, the existence of which you are forced to live with?
- reassessing the financial parameters of the book – i.e. costs and print run?
- taking advice from and informing colleagues about what was going on?
- conveying to the author an understanding of the seriousness of the situation from the house's point of view?
- getting the author on your side?
- keeping your colleagues on side?

An impossible job? 9

In this chapter we concentrate on particular aspects of handling the workload:

- inheriting other editors' lists
- managing email
- fear of failure

Anyone reading this book from cover to cover, with little prior knowledge of publishing, would wonder how editors ever sleep. There is so much to do and so much to fret about. Being an editor is a very difficult, but rewarding, job and there are indeed many editors who would rightly claim that they are not getting enough sleep. The pressure of work is intense, and seems increasingly so. All publishing houses are driven by growth for financial and strategic reasons. This is particularly so in the big houses where there is finance to support growth. Productivity and performance are constantly emphasised and scrutinised. It is actually quite difficult for new editors to go through a gradual process of development. Many are given a great deal of responsibility very quickly. These days even smaller independent houses need to put their editors under pressure.

The need for a combination of entrepreneurial drive, financial awareness, attention to detail, high productivity *and* social and psychological skills, all within a highly competitive market, is asking a lot of anyone. Not all editors can manage this load. As in other professions, people are sometimes recruited and promoted into jobs, who seem likely to be able to cope and do well but, in practice, are simply not good enough. It is difficult to judge properly just how good an editor is until his or her books are published and to measure, both in sales and in reviews, the editor's proficiency. Moreover, editors are required who are proficient over a sustained length of time.

Consistency of performance over time is what makes some editors valuable properties and what makes publishing houses fight to try to employ them and keep them. Times have changed and whereas in the past editors – recognised and appreciated in a publishing house, and appropriately rewarded – might spend the greater part of their working lives there, today they are more likely to move from job to job. Gone are the days when it would seem unthinkable for an editor to leave a particular publishing house because of the successful and intensely close relationship that the editor has had with that house and its authors. Editors move more frequently now because they are offered substantial salaries to do so, and as a result of the changing ownership and management of many houses in recent years. Many simply 'move on': they develop interests which they can pursue in other houses.

There has never been a time when editors were not expected to get through prodigious amounts of work. However, there have been two developments in recent years that have had a considerable effect on the way in which we function. The first concerns handling lists which you inherit from someone else. The second is managing email.

Publishing is less settled now than it used to be. Take-overs and mergers are part of business life. Also, stand-alone lists are frequently sold on by companies for whom they are no longer a good fit within their publishing houses.

INHERITING OTHER EDITORS' LISTS

Whether you are caught up in a take-over or a merger, or a list purchase, the chances are that you may find yourself being handed a list in which you had formerly played no part. Simply starting a new job and taking on someone else's list provides similar experiences. There are several consequences to this:

- Your workload now suddenly grows. It might even double.
- One positive construction to put on this is that overnight you may move from being an editor with responsibility of modest proportions to an editor with considerable power because of the size of the turnover you now handle. You move up the pecking order.
- Your visibility increases in the house. In your hands has been put a list that the company wanted to purchase. They may even have paid rather more than they needed, because they wanted it that badly. You will be under pressure to show that their investment was worthwhile.
- You have to bring yourself to a level of understanding and familiarity with the books purchased quite rapidly. You must do that if you are

to be an effective editor for them. This means not just the backlist but the forward commitments.

- You may, unhappily, discover that the books are not entirely to your liking. You would not be the first editor to grumble about the quality of books inherited. You may even be handling books that you had actually turned down for publication. One editor found herself inheriting an entire series which, when offered it some time earlier, she turned down because she thought that the series concept and the individual books on offer were badly focused and she had little confidence in either the series editor or the individual authors.
- Conversely, you may discover that you have been handed some gems of backlist and frontlist publishing. In which case, count yourself extremely lucky and be thankful.
- Whether you are happy or unhappy with your new books, you will also inherit a set of authors. Authors, with very few exceptions, thoroughly dislike being moved around from one publishing house to another, and by extension from one editor to another. You will now have to spend more time getting to know these authors, and you need to be alive to the fact that many of them will be looking for reassurance that their new home is a good place to be.
- Authors whom at first you might find difficult are those who in their previous houses were given perhaps rather too much latitude to become involved in publishing decisions to an extent that you believe to be professionally inappropriate. Guard against being told that the previous editor 'promised' this and 'promised' that. Unless these promises are in writing, there is no evidence.
- There are also authors who become very attached to their editors. It is of course what you want from your authors – the successful ones anyway – but you will have to deal with the consequences of their being forceably detached from an editor whom they trusted and rated highly.

THE WAY FORWARD

1 Be positive about what has happened. Management will not wish to hear that what they did was a bad idea. Yes, it is going to involve a lot more work for you but that does not mean that acquiring the list was a bad idea commercially speaking.
2 You may be fortunate in that management realises that your workload has leapt up and offers you an extra pair of hands to help you. If it does not, bide your time before asking for extra help. When you do, make sure you have prepared your ground thoroughly. Produce your figures for through-put showing not just the number of backlist

and frontlist titles for which you are responsible, but also the number of submissions coming to you during the course of the year. As a result of a consolidation of publishing in your hands, it is likely that you will be in receipt of more submissions. Hopeful authors have one less house to try. It is best to start this process with some informal discussions with your line manager, so that he or she is involved and in the picture. However, again, be positive.

3   In tandem with this information, provide a plan for what you can do with this much bigger list if you have more help. You are bound to come up with ideas for list development. Management will be pleased if you produce some constructive ideas for making the best of their acquisition.

4   Put aside – difficult though it is – negative perceptions about the books you have inherited. You must deal with them in the same professional way as you deal with books you contracted. You may find that the closer you get to them, the more you see their attractions. Even if you do not, at the very least, you have given of your professional best to each book. In fact, your professional best may strengthen those books' chances in the market-place.

5   Write to all the authors you have inherited immediately. Faced with writing a letter that has to go to anything between dozens and hundreds of authors, it is very easy to slip into 'official speak' – a letter that contains platitudes and is unlikely to grab the imagination of the recipients. Put yourself in the position of the authors. What would you like them to feel when they read that letter? What could you say that will make them feel that they are in a safe pair of hands? Give plenty of thought to that letter. Put something of yourself into it so that they have some sense of you. To use an old-fashioned expression – come across. You should of course offer to see authors recently under contract and in the process of writing, or those whose books are currently going through production.

6   Make a special effort with key authors and key series editors. Take them to lunch and work hard at getting to know them and involving them with what you are doing now and what your plans are for the list.

One final thought on this kind of experience. Look at it this way: to have a big list is what you planned; you've just got there earlier. If you had decided to try for another job – inevitably one that will mean a step up the ladder – this is the extent of responsibility you would get if you were given the job.

The difference is that growing a big list or applying for a more senior job would have been your choice. In this situation, you did not have a choice, but think carefully before claiming that this is not what you want at all.

MANAGING EMAIL

Email is a boon to publishers because it allows significant amounts of material to be transferred between various parties. It also provides a means of instant communication. When publishers and authors habitually communicated with each other through letters, there was an accepted understanding that either party would not necessarily receive instant replies. Letters could be put aside for a more convenient moment. Often that moment somehow did not present itself for weeks. Writing a letter requires more thought and effort. Emails can be dashed out, grammatical warts and all.

There is definitely still a place for the letter. Letters should be used for a formal or serious message. Moreover, we automatically keep copies of letters and we are able to refer to what was written if a difficult situation arises. Likewise, you should not delete email messages that are substantive in content, for the same reason. Ridding oneself of out-of-date email messages is a good practice, but think carefully before you press the delete button.

Email is brilliant for chasing authors for progress on their books. However, it should not be your sole mode of communication for authors who may want to ignore your enquiries. There is no substitute for meeting an author face-to-face or talking to him or her on the telephone if you are really anxious about keeping a delivery date and want to see or hear for yourself that the author is committed to it.

Email is also brilliant for contacting advisers, sending them book proposals, and having discussions about the material they are examining. It can speed up this process enormously.

Email can turn into a communication monster. A disciplined approach to email is required. During moments of boredom, *ennui* or when your brain is simply hurting, it is so easy to take a sneaky look into the email box to see if anything interesting has arrived. You should really be sticking to your original task, however much you would like to walk away from it. Here are some basic rules for handling email:

- Look at email when you first arrive in the office and see what has arrived overnight. Delete any emails that do not require action from you and whose content is not important.
- Answer messages whose replies can be dealt with by you instantly. It is important that you differentiate between emails that take no time at all to read and respond to and those that will need far more time to deal with and could make inroads into the list of priorities you have set yourself for the day.

- Attachments which need careful reading should be put aside to be looked at later in the day. If they need printing out, do it then, or ask your assistant to print them out for you if they are lengthy.
- Leave email aside until you have worked through some of the important tasks you have set for yourself. It might be best if you close email down for a while so that you are not tempted to answer any messages that come in.
- You can return to email later – perhaps at lunchtime, or when you have finished those 'must do' tasks.
- Everyone has had the experience of 'losing' an email because you have scrolled so far down the inbox that you can no longer see (and therefore be reminded of) the email that still has not been answered. It's a good policy to try to empty your inbox of everything that has been dealt with – either keeping a printed copy on file, or archiving it in a folder – so that you can keep your inbox relatively uncluttered and can always see unanswered messages on your screen.
- Do not use emails as your sole means of communicating with colleagues (apart from formal meetings). Remember you are working in a team and it helps to talk face-to-face.
- Do re-read your emails before you click the 'send' button. Although we have all become fairly accepting of the rather lax standards of writing that email somehow encourages because it is such an easy medium, perhaps authors are not the most suitable recipients of messages littered with spelling, punctuation and grammatical errors.

FEAR OF FAILURE

There are many things to come to terms with as an editor and an ever present threat is the prospect of failure. There is the big failure – 'I'm never going to become a real editor' – and the small failure – 'I'm terrified that this book is not going to be a success'. Experienced editors who have been in the business for a long time have probably by now (unless they are chronically anxious types) gone past the big failure stage but are perfectly capable of living constantly with the fear of the small failure: the book that mysteriously doesn't sell.

It would be wrong to give the impression of failure as a dominant force in an editor's life. There is much excitement and pleasure for those who can grasp the job properly. However, since fear of failure does loom large in the consciousness of many editors when they first begin their editorial career proper, it is worth examining in more detail what this anxiety is really all about, and how to come to terms with it and make it work positively.

AM I GOOD ENOUGH?

Wanting, and wanting very badly, to become an editor is a common enough emotion amongst newly recruited editorial staff. When ambition becomes reality, however, many young editors suddenly wake up to the realisation that the job is a highly responsible one and can be stressful. Not only is there a substantial workload to carry but the job requires indefinable qualities such as flair and judgement. With enough hours in the day you might just manage the workload, but anxiety sets in when questions about flair and judgement arise.

Nobody can teach flair, but with good training and support, a young editor can improve his or her judgement. Experience, of course, is the great teacher but the quality of your experience will also determine your approach to work.

There are gifted individuals who do seem to have extra special flair, perspicacity and judgement, but when, as a young editor, you see these abilities in play amongst older colleagues, you are not necessarily observing magic. You are witnessing experience. If you have learned well from experience, it builds confidence. These older editors are not doing their jobs effortlessly. Experience has taught them to work more confidently, decisively, and hence with an ease, even an elegance, which the younger editor craves. It is easy to jump to the conclusion that because someone (almost inevitably older) seems to have far less trouble grappling with all the risks and uncertainties of editorship, that person was somehow born to do the job; that it all comes perfectly naturally.

Most experienced editors will be quite candid about their mistakes. At this stage in their careers, of course, they can be candid because essentially they have demonstrated that they can acquire, commission and edit books. It is far more difficult to own up to mistakes when you have everything to prove.

Always remember that your editorial heroes will almost certainly have started out feeling the way you do: worrying how to sift the dross from the valuable in the pile of publishing proposals and typescripts that flood in. The worry cuts both ways: can I pick projects that will turn into good books; or will I turn down the ones that could be winners? Other typical worries are, how can I:

- find the right author for the brilliant idea I have?
- come up with a good idea to keep my successful author busy?
- go about finding a really good children's author and illustrator?
- anticipate the next trend which will help with my non-fiction list?
- repurpose our reference projects electronically?
- make our teaching materials for schools more competitive?

- turn my academic list into something more distinguished than that of my competitors?

It is best to face this procedural hurdle with a senior editor by your side. If your line manager has not already organised it, suggest regular meetings in which you can take him or her through the projects you want to pursue and those you wish to reject. Prepare for the meeting carefully, especially having marshalled your thoughts for and against proposals.

By going through this process, you can sort out your own ideas and also learn from the comments that the senior editor makes about content and market, about the choice of advisers, and you can often pick up other tips along the way. The senior editor also benefits from this kind of regular exchange. He or she can develop a good grasp of how you work so that you become much more of a 'known quantity'. Furthermore, sometimes new ideas can emerge from these sessions that the senior editor can pursue too.

Unfortunately it is not entirely unknown for senior colleagues to steal the ideas that junior colleagues have come up with and not give them the credit. There are no easy solutions to this problem. It is a risk you have to take, and if it does happen to you, find polite but firm ways of reminding that person of your part in the success and always agree the ideas that will be pursued by you and those he or she might want to follow through. Be assertive but not aggressive about this. No one likes being solemnly reproached. It may not have been your senior colleague's real intention to steal; more that their enthusiasm for something got the better of them.

Eventually you will feel less need for this regular interaction as it becomes clear that you are beginning to develop a sense of direction and confidence. At some point both parties will mutually agree that the time has come for you to work more autonomously, although there should always be a structure that allows for both parties to meet and discuss editorial matters on a more intermittent basis.

One thing should always be made clear from the start. What exactly is the manager expecting from you? That basically means agreeing targets, whether it is the number of titles, content or revenue. If you have a clear idea of what is expected then you have something to aim for.

WILL MY AUTHORS RESPECT ME?

The second major area that will tax all editors when they first start out is feeling confident in relation to the authors. Dealing with first-time, similarly nervous, authors seems less nerve-wracking than working with quite famous and successful ones. The truth is actually the reverse of this. Quite often it is the new authors who make the greatest demands on editorial skills simply because they are less confident about what they are doing. Experienced authors can often be 'hands off' and relaxed, allowing you the space to get on with your job.

You will eventually discover how each author works and wants to work with you. While there are certainly unpleasant ones amongst their ranks, authors are not nearly as frightening and forbidding as your fantasies depict them.

Authors are not looking for intellectual equals in their editors, or experts as well informed as they are. What they want in an editor is someone with whom they can feel comfortable and, more than anything else, someone who is competent at what they are doing. You may not be in a position yet to demonstrate that you have a complete grasp either of publishing or of the list on which you are working but by dealing with their concerns and their work promptly, efficiently and in a friendly and helpful way, you will go a long way in persuading them of the notion that they are 'in good hands'. That is the first and basic position to aim for and if you can do that on a sustained basis, you will find that confidence will gradually develop. Some editors find it a good tactic to admit that they know a little about a lot of things, which usually helps to explain gaps in their knowledge.

Remember that you are perfectly capable of holding intelligent conversations and discussions with your authors about the thing that really concerns them: the publication of their book. Over the years you will develop a sense of familiarity and expertise in your chosen field of publishing and may indeed turn out to be capable of discussing the subject you publish on a far higher level than when you started out. At that stage you have become highly effective: you not only understand and can carry out your publishing practice with skill but you have a good grasp of the subject matter and begin to enjoy discussing it with authors.

Never be afraid to admit to an author that you know very little about a particular aspect of a subject. It gives the author a chance to explain it to you, which he or she likes doing because it puts them in the position of being an expert. You can make up for your weakness in one direction by demonstrating your grasp of the area in which you are far more expert – publishing. Better to say, 'No, I don't know about that' than feign knowledge and inevitably be caught out looking foolish.

THE SMALL FAILURE

This is the book that fails to perform as well as you expected. It forms an inevitable part of your progress from inexperience to experience.

Everyone has them. If you have them regularly and cumulatively, however, you will be in trouble. Again, however, test reality. The chances are you work in a publishing house that has some system for approval of new projects. Whatever the tangible form that the system takes, it will almost certainly involve a thorough discussion among the members who meet to approve the project. It will most probably require evidence from past sales of fairly similar books, and it will require input from sales and marketing about the challenges that the book will present and whether they can be met. It will also require financial data – usually a projected profit-and-loss account for the book, perhaps including sales data for world-wide sales and subsidiary rights. Reports will probably be included from outside advisers if that is appropriate to the kind of publishing you are in. In sum, you will have done a great deal of preparatory work on the book to reach the point where you ask for approval. If you have done your work thoroughly and if your colleagues have done their work of evaluation thoroughly, you have no reason to fear that the book will be a failure.

There is one great exception to this. If you insist that a book is going to work when the general mood is cautious or pessimistic then you are taking a risk if you do insist on pushing for the book. If the ethos of your company is 'democratic', i.e. if the majority of the assembled colleagues do not want to support it, your book will get turned down. However, if you work for a company where the editor does have the last word, then the book will be contracted and you must remember that you have taken a risk. Its failure or success is going to be up to you, and you cannot complain if it does fail.

Every editor must occasionally be allowed to take such risks because it is a fact that many good books have been published solely because an editor was prepared to fight for them. But you are only as good as the last risk that worked!

DARK DAYS

Even highly experienced editors get dark days. Periods when no potentially successful books seem to be on the horizon and news from the sales department is not cheerful. There is no reason to assume that good publishing proposals should arrive in a regular fashion. As chance would have it, they often arrive in a rush – all at the same time – and then there will follow a period when you seem to have very little to propose for publication. That is simply the way it seems to happen and you certainly should not waste your time or your colleagues' time proposing books just for the sake of it. Try to subdue the sense of panic that inevitably ensues. If you are doing your job properly, assiduously making contacts with authors, advisers and agents, and following through, the proposals will eventually arrive too. They will not if you just sit back and worry.

There is one particular period made up of what seems like endless dark days. This is the period when you have signed up books but have yet to see them published. They are all still in the pipeline. You have yet to discover if you are capable of being an editor because there are no sales and no reviews as a measure of your judgement. There is no avoiding this. You need to find the courage to recognise the anxiety and stick to the task. Eventually, when the books become a reality, that long period will be over and you will be able properly to assess what you have achieved.

THE CHANGING CULTURE

Much emphasis has been laid on the importance of working with other people. One of the most significant changes in publishing practice over the years has been the gradual recognition that the close integration of all the departments in a publishing house is highly beneficial to good publishing. The need for integration and close working relationships also extends within the editorial departments. Editors who have been fortunate enough to be trained and managed by senior editors are likely to extend the same kind of support and sense of direction to the next generation of editors, when they have management responsibilities, and so on. The trouble with the so-called 'tough minded' view that young editors should be thrown in the deep end and made to get on with it, is that those same young editors may also end up perpetuating that view themselves.

Editors who have properly absorbed the cultural change towards teamwork will be more professional and confident as a result. They will regard the input of other colleagues as valid and necessary. They will understand and learn about the bigger picture – the whole house and how it functions, and how it functions within the broader publishing market – and as a result, become more effective editors.

THE BEST JOB?

Crossing the great divides between editorial, production and sales and marketing used to be comparatively rare. You started out in one department, learned your expertise, and stayed there. Today young people move around, especially from editorial to sales and marketing and vice versa, before finally settling on one or the other. In North America the principle of giving new entrants into publishing a good general training has been in operation for some time. In the UK some houses practise general training but most do not, although there is some evidence of that approach gaining ground here. •

Whatever your route to the job of editor is, you are facing a job that requires both craft and graft. Get to grips with that and you are doing a job that is rewarding, influential, full of variety and, above all, stimulating. It is a privileged position to be in. Not many can profess to such high job satisfaction. Talk to friends working in other jobs or professions and you will discover the extent of your privilege. Yes, long hours are required of you and, historically, salaries have not compared favourably with other professions.

Salaries are now beginning to rise, especially in the larger companies, where rewarding successful editors is seen as an important corollary of raising professional standards. Being 'in possession of a private income' is no longer one of the necessary attributes of an editor. Does it really matter if it is the best job in the house or not? Your colleagues in sales and marketing would be most likely to contest that view. And it depends on what you want out of publishing. If you want power, in addition to the ability to exercise your professional skills, perhaps you should have become a publishing accountant. It is probably a good reflection of the ways in which publishing has been transformed in recent years into a more commercial industry that such a lively debate can be guaranteed.

It was said at the very outset that being an editor is still to occupy the pivotal role. On these grounds alone, an editor can claim to be doing the best job. What makes being an editor so special within publishing and in relation to many professions, is that you have something tangible to show for your efforts. There is known to be a very high correlation between job satisfaction and the ability to see one's part in the production of something or a successful outcome.

A book is a culmination of many hands and heads working in complex ways. The outcome is a minor miracle for everyone involved to hold in their hands. But the editor can hold it and lay claim, more than anyone else except the author, to its very existence. That is satisfaction.

A future for the book? 10

Some readers will be asking themselves, why bother with all this detailed advice and instruction on how to edit books? The future lies in electronic publishing. Indeed there does seem to be a great future. On-line publishing is established, especially in academic, scientific and technical publishing. The e-book is still in development but there are many arguments about whether the market wants it.

However sceptical you are about all this, you cannot ignore it. But the range of copyright, pricing and cost implications is demanding for anyone trying to come to grips with the situation. Again, readers are recommended to read Lynette Owen's book *Selling Rights* to get an excellent summary of the many variations of digital publishing and their copyright, usage and cost implications. At the moment, digital publishing – for traditional book publishers – is still essentially a by-product of print publishing and, therefore, an issue for subsidiary rights activity.

Anyone exclusively reared on book reading as one of their main sources of education and leisure is always amazed by the enormous ease with which young children handle computers and videos. For anyone over the age of 40, television is something that was introduced into their lives – it was not always there – and for many, something they were allowed to view on a rationed basis. It can still remain mentally the thing that stands in the corner. Today's young children are at one with television and the video machine. In school they will have been trained to use computers as the development of a skill necessary for the workplace. Some will have received part of their education in the core curriculum via software packages. These young people are perfectly comfortable with the electronic age and it is inevitable that when they grow up and have spending power, they will want to buy their information and entertainment in a format that suits them.

A publisher who chooses to ignore that is therefore in danger of being left behind or having their publishing function gradually taken over by the software producers. It would be thoroughly foolish to suggest right now that the book is going to disappear. Books still have advantages over electronic products. They are very comfortable on the eye (and the back) for sustained use. They are very easy to carry around, user friendly and they don't need additional back-up. They are also cheap.

However, if you work in a large corporation, the chances are that you and your colleagues are being encouraged, or instructed, to work on electronic publishing ideas, including the repurposing of books into digital formats. There are some publishing houses who no longer see themselves as publishers but as 'information providers'. The chances still are that the majority of people choosing to work in publishing do so because they want to be publishers, not information providers. Such concepts will not bed down comfortably everywhere.

It is important to remember, faced with the new, that the publishing function is still the publishing function, whatever the media. You are still engaged in finding material people want to buy, which you package in a form they find attractive and comfortable to use; marketing it so they know it is available and how to get it; and pricing it at a level they are prepared to pay. Many of the processes described in this book remain essentially the same for the development of electronic products, even if content delivery is different. They are:

- market research
- product evaluation
- creative input
- design and production
- costings, revenue and profit
- sales and marketing

No one who has a grounded view of reality really knows what is going to happen with digital publishing, but in the meantime, far-sighted publishers will get on with it, positioning themselves for the future at no doubt considerable cost to their companies.

Many of them will be proved right because they will have done their groundwork properly. It is very easy to be tempted into digital products because 'it's the thing to be doing'. However, as has often been said, the invention of the printing press would have passed over into history unsung if (for social and cultural reasons) there had not arisen a demand for reading in a form that was more accessible and convenient than the illuminated manuscript. Books are one means of presenting information; digital products are another.

THE EXAMPLE OF CD ROMS

The CD Rom format has established itself. It is particularly useful for information and reference publishing, allowing very large amounts of content to be stored and to be manipulated by the user with ease. It can be updated relatively easily too and at a low cost to the producer. When the excitement of the possibilities that CD Rom presents hit the publishing business, it led to a number of large projects being developed for the consumer market, as well as the specialist markets. Huge amounts of money were spent to develop and produce CD Roms, on the assumption that individuals would pay up to £1,000 to buy one of these.

A perception emerged, which seemed to date from the early to mid-twentieth century, that there would be family demand for access to prodigious amounts of information, based on the encyclopaedia model. Encyclopaedias had been successful at that time because they plugged into growing affluence and increasing levels of aspiration within the population. They also succeeded at that time because the ordinary person was comparatively lacking in information. Television inevitably became the great information provider, and in turn has been almost superseded by the internet. The idea that families would have these CD Roms on a shelf, where they could be pulled down, shared and explored, was simply misplaced. Families, and individuals, could easily get their information elsewhere, and without being expected to part with hundreds of pounds.

What compounded the difficulty was that if an interested buyer went into a shop, saw a CD Rom and was tempted, there were scarcely any places where the CD could be demonstrated. There was little possibility of doing the equivalent of flicking through a book.

CD Roms are a very good example of a bright new tomorrow that did not work out quite the way the futurologists firmly predicted. Unfortunately, a lot of investment money was wasted as a result.

TECHNICAL AND DEVELOPMENT CHALLENGES FOR EDITORS

When faced with digital products, as well as taking yourself through the essential processes described above, bear in mind some other considerations.

The first is that you must familiarise yourself with the technical dimensions of the packages you are considering. This is one area where you cannot cut corners or expect that someone else down the corridor will know about it if you don't.

If you decide to go into partnership with a digital producer, how will that deal look in five years' time?

Specialist digital products often provide helplines for the buyer. Do you have the resources to provide one? Answering the telephone and dealing with users' problems is a time-consuming business and can be costly.

Marketing these products is likely to entail expensive promotion pieces and demonstrations. Pricing policies are particularly challenging. For consumer products the publisher has to guess in absolute terms what the ordinary buyer is prepared to pay. For specialist publishers there is the question of how to judge the pricing of the electronic version in relation to the print version.

There is so much to take on board that it is best to view all this as an opportunity to be involved in something that is demanding, exacting and exciting. Remember, however, in the excitement of developing something entirely new, to preserve some sense of detachment so that you can always apply those first principles of evaluation of your product and market. If you keep them in the forefront of everything you do, they will serve you well.

IN CONCLUSION

Before digital publishing becomes a mature business – and we are some way off from that – in a period of uncertainty, ask yourself constantly: 'Because we have the technical means to do something, *should* we do it?' If you are busily persuading yourself to develop and produce something because the technical means of handling that new product are so impressive – so flexible, so easy to manipulate and cross refer (just a few key strokes!) – then you may be losing sight of your business. No one buys a book just because it is easy to turn the pages. It is the combination of content and page-turning that has made the book so successful. Beware, therefore, of simply trying to sell means, without ends. 'Ends' for our purposes is content, which somebody wants. Make sure that your content and your means of delivery make a happy marriage. Always ask yourself the following questions:

* Is there a market for this product, and why?
* Do I have the expertise to make this product?
* Can I produce it at a price that the market will bear?
* Do I know how to reach the market with this product?
* Will there be a satisfactory relationship between my costs and my revenue?
* Can I use digital formats to create products that will complement my paper products?

These are the same questions you should ask yourself as a book editor. Therefore, do not be frightened when faced with ambitious plans for digital product development, and do not be frightened to ask the same questions of management.

Finally, do not allow yourself to go down the either/or road. It is not a matter of the book versus digital publishing. Your job is essentially about gathering, ordering and delivering content. Choose your method of content delivery to suit the best use that can be made of it.

Recommended reading and other resources 11

Any aspiring editor should read the *Bookseller* and *Publishing News* from cover to cover every week. The *Bookseller* also has a very useful website where you can find other news items, information and articles. Editors who have a professional interest in the North American market should read *Publishers' Weekly* on a regular basis.

Below is a list of books which should be read in conjunction with this book. The list is short but the books are tried and tested.

Athill, Diana (2001) *Stet*. London: Granta Books
Baverstock, Alison (1997) *Marketing Books*. London: Kogan Page
Blake, Carole (1999) *From Pitch to Publication*. London: Macmillan
Butcher, Judith (1993) *Copy Editing* (3rd edn). Cambridge: Cambridge University Press
Clark, Giles (2000) *Inside Book Publishing* (3rd edn). London: Routledge
Epstein, Jason (2001) *Book Business: Publishing Past, Present and Future*. London: W. W. Norton
Hurst, Christopher (2002) *The Invisible Art*. London: C. Hurst
Jones, Hugh and Benson, Chris (2002) *Publishing Law*. London: Routledge
Owen, Lynette (2001) *Selling Rights* (4th edn). London: Routledge
Owen, Lynette, ed. (2002) *Clark's Publishing Agreements* (6th edn). London: Butterworth LexisNexis
Peacock, John (1995) *Book Production* (2nd edn). London: Chapman & Hall
Randall, G. (2002) *Principles of Marketing*. London: Thomson Learning
Woll, Thomas (1999) *Publishing for Profit*. London: Kogan Page

In addition, anyone who can steal, beg, borrow, or – with luck – buy a copy from a second-hand bookseller with a website of out-of-print books, should read Jeremy Lewis's *Kindred Spirits: Adrift in Literary London*. Better still, HarperCollins, under whose Flamingo imprint it first appeared, should reprint it. This book is an urbane and often hilarious account of book publishing as it used to be. Packed with eccentricity, bad behaviour and publishing vision/obstinacy/single-mindedness, it paints a picture of a world that many people, still, think they might be entering.

OTHER RESOURCES

There are two organisations which provide excellent opportunities for editors to meet each other and also provide events and training:

- The Society of Young Publishers: www.thesyp.demon.co.uk
- Women in Publishing: www.cyberiacafe.net/wip

Sources for training and education in publishing are many and various. They include the Publishing Training Centre, generally recognised as the industry leader, which runs a wide range of courses at various levels throughout the year.

Courses within higher education institutions are also numerous. Those offering postgraduate degrees in publishing – some of which also offer education in electronic publishing – are:

- City University
- The London Institute
- Loughborough University
- Napier University
- Oxford Brookes University
- Robert Gordon University
- University of Stirling

The websites for these organisations will contain full information on what is on offer.

For a full list of sources for training, see the 'Appendix' in Giles Clark's *Inside Book Publishing*.

Index